Housing
by Lifestyle

McGraw-Hill Books of Related Interest

Housing by Lifestyle

The Component Method of Residential Design

James W. Wentling

Second Edition

McGraw-Hill, Inc.

New York   San Francisco   Washington, D.C.   Auckland   Bogotá
Caracas   Lisbon   London   Madrid   Mexico City   Milan
Montreal   New Delhi   San Juan   Singapore
Sydney   Tokyo   Toronto

Library of Congress Cataloging-in-Publication Data

Wentling, James W.
    Housing by lifestyle : the component method of residential design
/ James W. Wentling.—2nd ed.
        p.   cm.
    Includes bibliographical references and index.
    ISBN 0-07-069293-9 (acid-free)
    1. Architecture, Domestic—United States—Designs and plans.
2. Room layout (Dwellings)—United States—Designs and plans.
I. Title.
NA7205.W46   1995
720'.973—dc20   94-23192
                                                            CIP

    2 3 4 5 6 7 8 9 0   DOC/DOC   9 9 8 7 6 5

ISBN 0-07-069293-9

*The sponsoring editor for this book was Joel Stein, the editing supervisor was
Jane Palmieri, and the production supervisor was Pamela Pelton. It was set in
Century Schoolbook by McGraw-Hill's Professional Book Group composition unit.*

Printed and bound by R. R. Donnelley & Sons Company.

42.25
DEC97

Contents

Preface to the Second Edition

Although it has been only some five years since the first writing of *Housing by Lifestyle*, much has changed in the housing industry. In the early 1990s, housing production declined to postwar lows in response to a very deep recession. The economic euphoria of the go-go eighties evolved into the modest and frugal nineties. Price escalations and the appreciation of residential real estate leveled off, and some areas even saw deflation in home prices. Therefore, people's attitudes about housing, along with other consumer products, became more conservative.

Housing design inevitably is linked to social change. Residential designs are evolving constantly to reflect the current values and needs of society. Today those values include practicality, security, affordability, and environmental responsibility, along with the enduring needs for comfort and livability. Concerns for "green" and "healthy" housing have come to the forefront in the minds of most consumers. Buyers today anticipate staying in their homes for a longer period of time, as evidenced by the surge of activity within the remodeling industry.

Meanwhile, expanding technologies are continuing to influence how our society lives and works. For a simple example, most of the drawings in this edition of *Housing by Lifestyle* are computer generated, compared to the all hand-drawn graphics of the first edition, published only five years ago. These same technologies are turning our homes into electronic castles, filled with media devices and connections to the rest of the world through telecommunication options now available on the so-called "information highway."

Therefore, a second look at the principles of the initial edition of *Housing by Lifestyle* seemed warranted. The text and graphics have been modified to respond to the current economic and social conditions. Most of the original principles need only modification, however, because despite constantly changing social values, the basic program for lifestyle design remains linked to people—who do change their values, but still require and enjoy basic comfort and livability in their homes.

James W. Wentling

Preface to the First Edition

Whether for the large-production builder or the entrepreneur building only a few homes each year, design quality has always been integral to successful home building. This book will review design issues that currently face members of the home-building community and will also address the concerns of other kinds of readers. Realtors, appraisers, and lending officials can benefit from an explanation and illustration of residential design movements. Consumers of housing—those who contemplate building their own home, purchasing a new home, or remodeling the one they already have—can help ensure its long-term resale value by obtaining updated information on design trends that affect housing.

Housing by Lifestyle is based on the theory that we spend our time at home in very different "component" areas. A component includes a series of rooms that naturally work in concert with one another. In a midsized house, for example, the kitchen, breakfast area, and family room make up what is called the community component, the primary location within the home for group activities and gatherings. The privacy, ceremonial, functional, and outdoor components will also be defined.

The text will review how the various components of a home can be organized in relation to one another for maximum livability. It will profile popular features and options that stimulate buyer interest and compare the historical and evolving roles of typical rooms within each component.

In the future, lifestyle concerns, demographic shifts, and settlement patterns will continue to alter our concept of house and home. This book attempts to preview where we are going.

Acknowledgments

Although many individuals merit acknowledgment for their assistance with this book, my current and past clients deserve initial recognition. I have found home builders to be excellent educators of residential designers, always eager to share the wealth of their knowledge on buyer preferences, market trends, and shifting lifestyle tastes. It is from this partnership of builder and designer that produces quality residential designs for consumers of housing.

Individual recognition must first go to Rebecca Hardin of Open Line for giving the original text a balanced perspective. Through her editorial guidance we produced a more readable and interesting manuscript. Debbie Curtis assisted with the revised text and graphic revisions, and Raymond Hale also assisted with the revised and new graphics. Joel Stein of McGraw-Hill provided advice and guidance from the formative stages of the concept of this book through its completion.

Finally and most important, I would like to thank my wife Anne for supporting my efforts, despite the many hours taken from our family time during the writing, editing, and production of *Housing by Lifestyle*.

Programming Housing for Contemporary Lifestyles

I once attended a seminar on trends in hotel design. To emphasize the philosophical changes in the lodging industry, one hotel operator remarked, "Ladies and gentlemen, we're not in the hospitality business—we're in the *entertainment business!*"

For similar reasons, those of us in the home building industry are in the midst of a comparable transformation. We are no longer merely providers of shelter. We are producers of *lifestyle-oriented environments.*

A variety of factors has brought about this change, including the following trends:

1. The average American household is shrinking, and is now down to 2.3 persons per household. This means that the need for *pure space* in a home is diminishing in importance. Instead, the emphasis is now on *how the space is programmed with features* to enhance the livability and enjoyment of the home.

2. Household compositions are also changing. The traditional family of Mom, Pop, and Kids is shrinking both in size *and* as a percentage of total U.S. households—with only 25 percent of all households now considered "traditional." Conversely, the percentage of "nontraditional" household groups— married adults without children, single parents, persons living alone, and

unrelated people sharing housing—has increased. Even many "traditional" households now contain diverse members that may range from infants
to teenagers, or grown children living at home, extended families, or combined households. (Figures 1.1 and 1.2)

Figures 1.1 (left), 1.2 (right)   Meet today's consumers of housing; they're smaller in household size and more
diverse in their lifestyle needs.

3. Employment trends have changed. The number of married households
    with both spouses working currently stands at 50 percent, and no longer
    is the male always the dominant breadwinner. Corporate downsizing has
    shifted jobs into smaller businesses, often requiring people to work part-
    time with flexible schedules or work at home. Innovations in technology
    and communications have made the central workplace less necessary,
    calling into question the need for expending massive amounts of energy in
    daily commuting. Therefore, *a portion of the home is becoming an exten-
    sion of the workplace,* while *time for home maintenance is diminishing*
    from people's schedules.

4. Personal values are changing also. Although more households include two
    working spouses, education, leisure, and cultural pursuits are often rated
    higher in priority than career advancement. The relative importance of
    family and individual relationships is increasing, while the "career
    advancement at all costs" value is waning. This means that *people want to
    spend more time in the comfort and security of a well-designed home envi-
    ronment.*

All of these trends are redefining how new housing is being programmed,
designed, and marketed. Increasingly, the decision to purchase a new home is
based primarily on *lifestyle considerations,* along with financial and locational
concerns. Because of these lifestyle considerations, home-buyer expectations
are markedly different from those of the postwar era.

During that period, home builders could primarily sell square footage; today, they must emphasize *design features* and *amenities*. Designs with style, drama, and flexibility have increased in number compared to traditional floor plans. Like the automobile industry, the housing market is now controlled by buyers looking for *specialized products*; instead of cookie-cutter houses, they want floor plans that reflect and accommodate their particular lifestyles.

This emphasis on *lifestyle-oriented design,* serving a wide range of households types, has inspired me to think of houses as an *assemblage of components,* with each component planned differently for each household type. As used in this book, the word "component" does not refer to prefabricated construction, but rather to a general area of a home based on its principal use. The analysis of homes as *components for living* often joins rooms that are used in concert. Rooms that fulfill the need for privacy are separated. Some rooms are treated as formal stage sets, whereas others reflect their informal, behind-the-scenes function. (Figure 1.3)

COMPONENT BLOCKS FOR MATURE FAMILY HOUSEHOLD

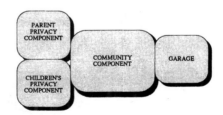

COMPONENT BLOCKS FOR YOUNG SINGLE PARENT HOUSEHOLD

COMPONENT BLOCKS FOR "MINGLES" HOUSEHOLD

Figure 1.3 Component design organizes the rooms of a home into component spaces which are assembled and fine-tuned to serve the needs of specific household types.

The Triumph of Style Over Structure

Historically, residential design has been dominated by *structural considerations*. From the simple log cabin to the elaborate estate home, internal spaces generally were established by framing spans of available structural materials. Therefore, houses typically have been defined as a series of rooms separated by load-bearing walls. Each room had a singular purpose, and was connected to other rooms by wall openings or circulation spaces. Accommodating programmed rooms within standard framing patterns often created unusual room dimensions and tenuous spatial relationships. It was also common for exterior designs to dictate or compromise the interior floor plan. (Figure 1.4)

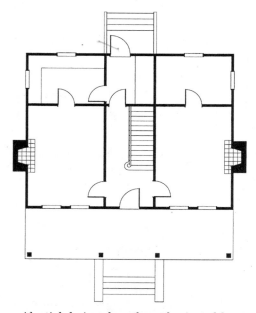

Figure 1.4 Historically, residential designs have been dominated by structural considerations; rooms were defined by load-bearing walls located according to the framing spans of available materials.

By contrast, today's home builders are adapting their designs to balance lifestyle demands with structural concerns. They talk about *sight lines* and *space flow* along with framing spans and insulation values. *Quality of space* is being emphasized along with *quantity of space*. Some builders are referring to their new homes as *lifestyle-adapted products*.

One can see two design movements in new residential communities—*transitional* and *traditional*. *Transitional design* is a term for the more contemporary approach to residential design and styling. It departs from historical traditions and explores new plan arrangements and facade treatments. *Traditional design,* on the other hand, appeals to more conservative tastes. It reaffirms values from the past, although it also incorporates contemporary trends in a more tempered fashion. (Figures 1.5 and 1.6)

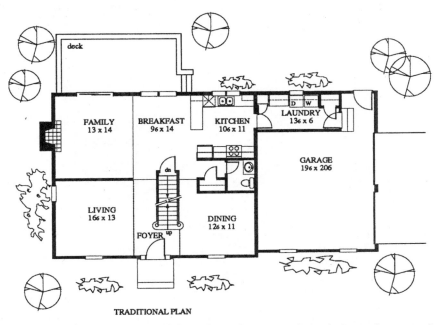

FAMILY
13 x 14

BREAKFAST
96 x 14

KITCHEN
106 x 11

LAUNDRY
136 x 6

GARAGE
196 x 206

LIVING
166 x 13

DINING
126 x 11

FOYER

TRADITIONAL PLAN

Figure 1.5 New homes with traditional floor plans adopt regional circulation and room configurations. In this Northeastern plan, the center-hall staircase arrangement with rooms on either side has been popular since colonial times.

Figure 1.6 New homes with traditional exteriors include regional styling, materials, windows, colors, and details. They may be replications of historical architectural styles, such as this brand-new bungalow-style house.

Progressive builders are constructing houses with transitional designs that include open spaces—with rooms that flow together, defined by low partitions, decorative columns, see-through fireplaces, and other elements. Upper-floor lofts overlook two-story rooms below. Cathedral ceilings are punctuated by skylights, dormers, and plant shelves. Internal spaces are virtually exploding from their previously rectangular confines. (Figures 1.7 and 1.8)

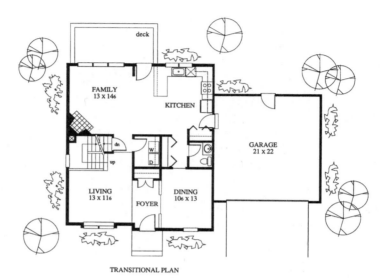

TRANSITIONAL PLAN

Figure 1.7 New homes with transitional floor plans experiment with new spatial relationships, and generally include extensive volume space, alternate stair configurations, combined rooms, and other progressive design concepts.

Figure 1.8 Within transitional floor plans, internal spaces are virtually exploding from their previously rectangular confines.

Houses based on *traditional designs* are constructed with an emphasis on quality, craftsmanship, and historical precedent. Their details and materials recall an earlier era: Interior moldings are becoming standard features again; marble vanities, hardwood floors, and custom cabinets are frequently specified; designs for ground-floor rooms are including 9- or 10-foot-high ceilings with oversized windows.

These gradual shifts in design philosophy in the home-building industry reflect a fundamental change in priorities that have reigned for centuries. *Lifestyle values* are taking precedence over *ease of construction. Style* is now triumphant over *structure.*

New Households = New Housing Designs

Accompanying this emphasis on style is the knowledge that today's housing consumers are an increasingly *segmented* lot. As mentioned earlier, traditional households (Mom, Pop, and Kids) continue to shrink in both average household size *and* as a percentage of our overall household population. Although the nuclear family remains the dominant household group in the housing market, it is not growing.

Nontraditional households, including childless couples, single parents with children, people living alone, and with roommates, now comprise 74 percent of all U.S. households. These groups are projected to account for most of the increase in households into the next century. As a result, the average household size declined in 1991 to a new low of 2.3 persons per household. (Figures 1.9 and 1.10)

Figures 1.9 (left), 1.10 (right) The average American household is shrinking, and is now down to 2.3 persons per household. Nontraditional households—couples without children, singles, and single parents—have increased. (*Figure 1.10 courtesy VSD Communications, Inc.*)

Market segmentation often has been described as a means of sustaining growth in the face of reduced demand. This definition applies to the home-building industry. Growth in the U.S. population continues to be flat, with less than a 1 percent increase projected for 1995.

To sustain growth, home builders have turned to market research to focus on shifts within the national population that may define new groups—*target markets*—who are narrowly defined by age, marital status, household income, and working habits. Several popular identifications of these groups include:

Empty Nesters: Mature couples whose children have grown up and moved out of the house.

Never Nesters: Couples who do not have children. Includes people of various ages.

Mingles: Unrelated single individuals sharing a residence. Also includes varied age categories.

Singles: Single people of various ages who live alone.

Single-Parent Households: One adult and one or more children of various ages.

In addition to the five basic categories of household composition, there are other differences among buyer groups that provide an overlay of further preferences in housing design. These include *region, household income, age, occupation,* and *behavior/values.* The latter category has been the subject of much research by market specialists, who have developed psychoanalytical classifications of people into groups such as *achievers* or *sustainers,* to further anticipate their design preferences.

Indeed, *market segmentation* has become a major force in the housing market. Home builders must now identify lifestyle preferences along with the buying power of their potential buyers before programming plans and amenities for their new houses.

Increased Land Costs = Smaller Lots and New Housing Types

Along with market segmentation, *rising land costs* have had a significant influence on new home designs. During the late 1980s, higher land and improvement costs prompted home builders to increase densities and introduce a host of new house/lot patterns for single-family detached homes. These new products included *"Z-lots, zipper-lots,* and *wide–shallow lot"* schemes—some of which have increased density yields up to about 10 units per acre but raised new questions about the quality of the resulting streetscape and neighborhood. (Figures 1.11 and 1.12)

While residential lots were becoming smaller, the average interior square footage of houses was increasing. The median square footage of new detached housing continued to rise to 2095 square feet in 1992, up from 1762 square feet in 1987, reflecting the dominance of the affluent, move-up buyers who

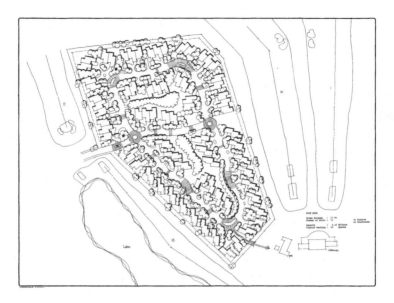

Figures 1.11 (top), 1.12 (bottom) In response to increased land costs, higher-density land planning has had a dramatic impact on housing designs—and not always in a positive manner. The facades on these high-density, zero-lot-line homes make the street look like a back alley.

demanded increased square footage. Therefore, we see a trend: Builders are constructing larger homes on smaller lots.

Smaller lots seem to suit the needs of lifestyle-oriented consumers of housing. There is plenty of evidence that today's buyers accept smaller lots because they mean *less yard maintenance*. There are even some cases where high-density detached housing was built with the land area around the homes fully maintained by a homeowner association. These "not-lots" have been marketed and sold in some areas of the country.

The New Lifestyle Concerns

What are these *new lifestyle concerns* we are referring to, and how are they influencing the housing market so strongly? With the rise of market segmentation, lifestyle preferences are helping to further define the new households. For example, while empty nesters may stress formal, contained spaces for entertainment, singles generally favor informal, open plans, and mingles may be most interested in plans with private and semiprivate domains. Regardless of the plan preferences of each consumer segment, the following seem to be common design preferences among all household groups:

Homes for Casual Living.   Households in general are looking for comfortable, informal spaces for living. People are living more informally today than a generation ago, and they have even less need for the formal parts of the home. Family rooms and kitchens are now more important than formal living and dining rooms. People want expanded space in the areas where they spend the bulk of their time.

Homes as Showcases.   The desire to use the home as a means of expressing wealth and/or social status is not new, but the demand for the incorporation of drama, style, and individuality into smaller and more affordable homes is of new and major significance in the housing market. Consumers of housing are making new demands for higher quality in finishes and craftsmanship. As the financial commitment of home ownership continues to increase, so will the demand for designs that are a showcase for one's possessions.

Homes with Upgraded Kitchens and Baths.   New attitudes about food and health have given more emphasis to kitchen and bath design in both large and small homes. Kitchen duties are more often shared, and the kitchen now is as much a social center as a functional one. Bathrooms have expanded to reflect people's interest in exercise and body care, again transforming a utilitarian space into a more gracious area.

Compartmentalized Homes.   Contemporary households value and express the need for both gathering places and spaces for individual retreat. The vast diversity in many contemporary households, which may include extended families or blended families, indicates a need to provide varied spaces within the home. The potential expandability and flexibility of floor plans are important to most new home buyers. Designs with multifunctional spaces that provide alcoves within common areas are also desirable.

Home as a Retreat.   In another time, the "home as castle" dream could be satisfied by a roof that didn't leak, a fireplace that didn't smoke, and a door that could be locked at night. Today the protection people want most is from *stress found in their daily lives*—traffic jams, waiting in lines, noise, and a general sense of being crowded, pushed, and shoved. In a world where nothing seems to work, people now view their home as a place of solace. Homeowners most often want to seek respite from the harried public realm by retreating into the comfort and security of their homes. (Figure 1.13)

Figure 1.13   Today's home buyers are looking for designs that provide comfortable, relaxed spaces for casual living.

Home as an Investment.   Homes are bought and sold according to *perceived value* and perceived *resale* value. Realtors are constantly reminding buyers that purchasing a home is generally the largest and most important investment a household will ever make. The prevailing wisdom is that a home will be one of our safest investments, a nest-egg of savings that will accrue from payments during the term of a mortgage. Perceived value is thus a critical element of contemporary housing, and to a greater degree than ever, this value will be measured by *design quality.*

The Five Component Areas

The *component method of design* provides a broad framework for achieving the above-described lifestyle objectives. Let's begin with a brief description of the five component areas found in an average American home.

Surveys indicate the average house to be in the 2000 square foot range, with three to four bedrooms and two-and-a-half bathrooms. Like the bulk of our national housing stock, it sits on a lot in a freestanding condition and includes a garage. Within the lot and house are the following five component areas:

Community component

This area is commonly thought of as being the *living* and/or the *family room*; however, the community component also includes the *kitchen* and an informal eating space, typically known as the *breakfast area.* Here, members of the household can be together and comfortably interact with one another in a relaxed setting. (Figure 1.14)

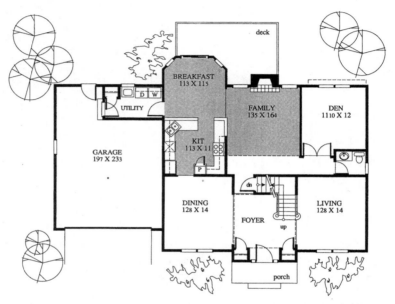

Figure 1.14 The *community component* includes the rooms where household members can be together in a relaxed setting.

Without a doubt, the community component spaces are the most important in the house. This is where the day-to-day drama of family life takes place. News is exchanged; announcements are made; fun occurs. This is the place to take off your shoes, relax, and let your hair down. No formalities exist. This is backstage.

Privacy component

Just as important as the need to come together is the need people have to be alone, private, and reflective. The *bedrooms* and *den,* or *library* satisfy this role in a typical home. Here, individuals can retreat from the larger group for some degree of peace and quiet. (Figure 1.15)

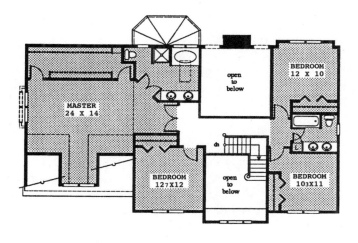

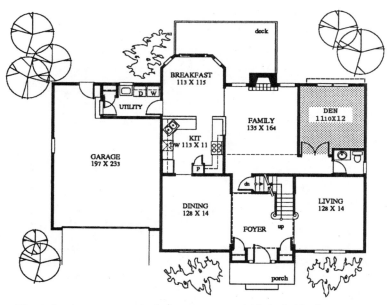

Figure 1.15 The *privacy component* includes rooms to which individuals can retreat from the larger group, to find some degree of peace and quiet.

As privacy areas, these rooms must be located separately, away from the community component and away from each other. Within most houses, the privacy component includes a *master bedroom* and *secondary bedrooms.* Larger homes may also have a *guest suite* and/or a *den, library, study,* or *home office,* all of which need maximum privacy.

Ceremonial component

Spaces to receive and entertain guests are a program requirement of most houses. Holiday gatherings, parties, and other social events demand rooms with a sense of formality and elegance. In larger homes, the *living* and *dining* areas fall into this category. Often decorated as showcases, these rooms are important, despite their infrequent use. Although formal dining may occur only several times a year, having ceremonial space for such occasions does enhance the idea that these meals are special.

The combination of the living room, dining room, and *entry hall foyer* defines the home's ceremonial component. The entry hall makes the all-important first impression on visitors and immediately conveys to the visitor the tone of the homeowner's style. The ceremonial component allows for the receiving hosts to extend a positive impression of their home to guests, and to entertain visitors in a formal setting. (Figure 1.16)

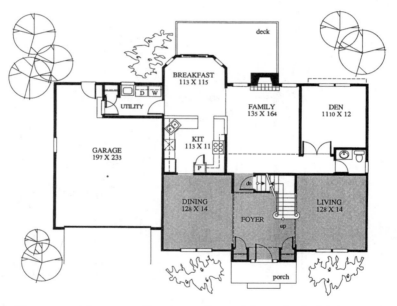

Figure 1.16 The *ceremonial component* has spaces for receiving and entertaining guests.

Functional component

Houses must also have room for all the requirements of an operational household. This means that space must be included for activities like washing clothes, mechanical areas, and storage for the devices most households use: automobiles, recreational equipment, and tools for general repair and maintenance. Here, functionality and utilitarian concerns dominate over aesthetics. This component generally includes *closets, attics, utility rooms, workshops, garages,* and (sometimes) *basements,* along with other practical areas of the home. Although not seen by guests, these spaces are equally important to the design of a livable home and merit careful design attention to ensure proper size and layout. (Figure 1.17)

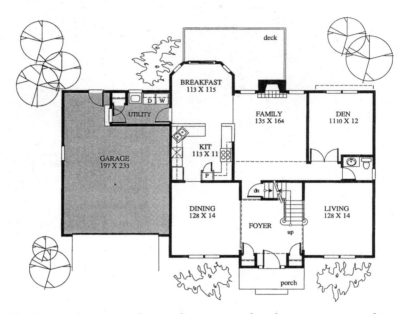

Figure 1.17 The *functional component* houses the storage and work spaces necessary for an operational household.

Outdoor component

In addition to all the internal spaces of a typical home, we must consider the exterior design of the house, along with the outside lot and yard areas. The outdoor component has several aspects, including *yards, gardens, patios, and decks,* as well as *building facades.* The design of the public area of a house and lot should reflect a friendly attitude toward the neighborhood and community, while the rear yard area is the place where occupants can relax without public scrutiny. This exterior duality recalls the community–privacy balance inside the home. Ceremony dominates the front, and functionality the rear. (Figure 1.18)

Figure 1.18 The *outdoor component* includes the land surrounding the home, exterior facades, landscaping, and accessory structures.

The Synthesis Process

Assembling the varied components into a workable design requires a true balancing act. Besides component relationships, the plan must incorporate current structural technology. Materials must be applied logically to allow the house to be built and sold within a competitive marketplace. Quality residential design must achieve a proper balance between style and pragmatism. (Figure 1.19)

Figure 1.19 Component design recognizes the need to achieve a balanced house design, from both an interior and exterior perspective.

   Within each of the following chapters, we'll explore a wealth of specific considerations and analyze each component in detail. We will also provide more specifics on the varied household *buyer profiles,* explaining their impact on each component. We'll also illustrate some of the ways component sizes and relationships can be fine-tuned so that the house correctly addresses the targeted buyer profile.

   A separate chapter will be devoted to *multifamily housing*; it will include examples of component modifications for higher-density attached housing. Finally, we will discuss the shift in *personal values* that is influencing diverse aspects of life in America, and the effect these changing values are having on planning and designing today's houses, as well as the influence they will exert on the shapes and forms of tomorrow's residential communities.

2

The Community Component: Kitchen, Breakfast Area, and Family Room

Our culture is dominated by food and infatuated with eating, and the domestic environment reflects this emphasis. Almost anyone in the home-building community will agree that the *kitchen* is the most important space in a typical house. The kitchen is also the pivotal element within the community component, because it also is the "nerve center" of the entire house. (Figure 2.1)

In today's kitchen, food preparation is only one of the activities that need to be provided for. The kitchen is also the primary social center of most homes. Whether for the formal entertainment of guests or the day-to-day exchanges of family life, the kitchen serves as a backdrop for constant social activity. This fact is mirrored in the many television shows that invariably use the kitchen as a primary stage set to document the fictional household's daily activities.

Most kitchen areas are incomplete without an informal eating area, commonly known as the *breakfast room*. This is really a misnomer, because lunches, dinners, coffee breaks, and snacks are taken here as well. It is also a social area where much conversation occurs. By contrast, the formal dining

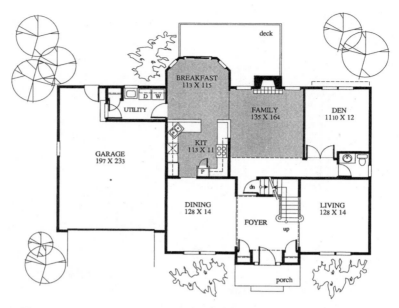

Figure 2.1 The community component includes the kitchen, an informal dining or "breakfast" area, and an informal living space, generally the family room.

room is reserved for special occasions. The informal eating area is therefore part and parcel of the overall kitchen design. (Figure 2.2)

In larger houses, the kitchen/breakfast area spills over into the *family room,* to complete the community component. (Figure 2.3) The design of this combined area generally is oriented towards a deck or patio with yard access, which then fully encompasses the informal areas where households spend most of their time. (Figure 2.4) In a well-designed home, these environs all work in concert with each other to maximize comfort, livability and the sheer enjoyment of living.

Market surveys have shown that 80 percent of home buyers prefer that the rooms of the community component (kitchen, breakfast and family) face the rear of the lot. The preference seems to say two things: (1) a rear orientation is desirable because it adds *privacy* for casual gatherings and relaxed household activities, and (2) rooms that define the community component should be *physically connected,* since their common usage logically links them together. Floor plans that emphasize these rooms in terms of optimal location, configuration, and spatial flow between one another, hold great appeal to most home buyers and are actively sought in all markets.

Design of the community component—kitchen, breakfast, and family rooms—should also acknowledge that in the lifestyle of most households, the traditional sit-down family meal has been replaced by the *grazing* concept. It's true—household eating patterns have changed. Rather than eating a family meal with all household members seated together, many people now eat

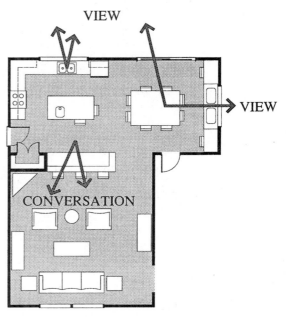

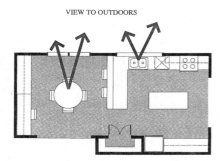

VIEW TO OUTDOORS

Figure 2.2 The kitchen and breakfast area should be designed to work together as a unit, with both spaces having generous access to light and views.

Figure 2.3 In larger homes, the kitchen and breakfast area generally open into a family room, all of which should work together as a component space.

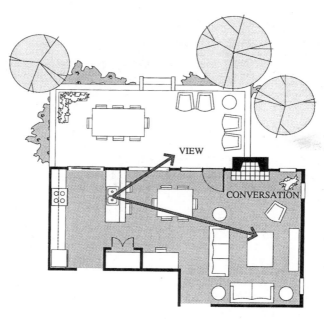

Figure 2.4 The community component should have convenient access to outdoor living spaces such as a patio, deck, lanai, screened porch, or sunroom.

individually by *grazing,* eating very simple meals or snacks at different times and in varying locations throughout the community component.

A good relationship among the rooms of the community component will accommodate these casual eating patterns. For example, kitchens should include some open counter space that can also be used for bar-type seating or as a place to eat while standing. Providing an *island counter* in the kitchen design is an ideal way to satisfy the casual-eating phenomenon, as is the *peninsula* or *bar* counter; both solutions provide household members with varied locations to select for *casual eating while socializing* in the community component. (Figure 2.5) The family area should also be designed to allow comfortable arrangements for informal dining, with dimensions that allow for flexible seating patterns. As with the breakfast area, easy access to the kitchen is important.

Each space within the community component has its own specific requirements as well. A review of the more detailed design considerations for each includes the following:

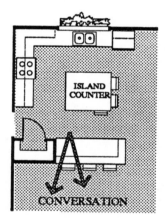

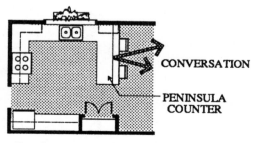

Figure 2.5 Both the "island" and "peninsula" kitchen counter configurations are currently very popular because of more casual household eating patterns.

Kitchen

Within the last half-century, the kitchen has evolved from a small, utilitarian space into the most important room in the house. As a result of this evolution, the kitchen has also become the most difficult room to design. Kitchen layouts must anticipate complex circulation issues, both within the kitchen and in its accessibility to the dining room, entry, garage, and outdoor dining areas. The kitchen must also physically relate to the breakfast area and family room/great room. Most importantly, kitchen design must incorporate access to views, natural light, and ventilation.

The functional design of counter space, cabinets, and storage within the kitchen is critical. Major appliances must be located next to adequate counter space. Both upper and lower-cabinet storage is needed. The clearances between counters must be comfortable, and shelving should be distributed throughout. (Figure 2.6) Now let's get even more specific about kitchen design issues:

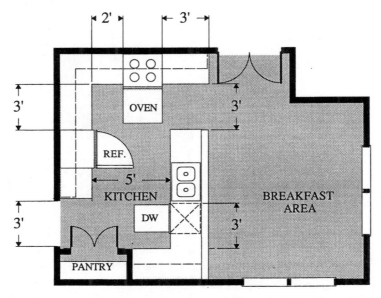

Figure 2.6 Proper clearances between counters and appliances are critical to achieving a functional kitchen layout.

The sink is the most important appliance in the kitchen. As the principal workstation, the sink is the place where occupants most often stand. It is therefore very desirable to *provide a view in front of the sink*. Ideally, this is an outside window; however, it may be an internal view, generally to the breakfast area or family room beyond. (Figure 2.7)

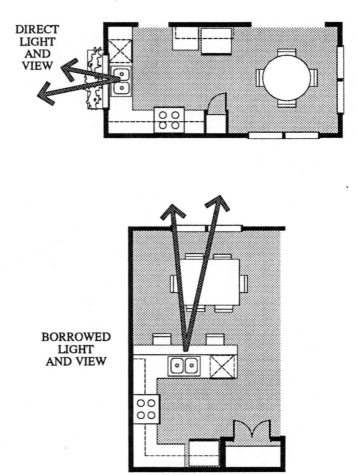

Figure 2.7 Windows in the kitchen are most desirable directly in front of the sink. If that can't be done, it may be possible to "borrow" light and views from an adjacent area.

The sink needs *plenty of counter space* on either side, with 2 to 3 linear feet considered ideal. Further, the *dishwasher* (a new appliance 30 years ago, now considered standard kitchen equipment) must be accessible to the sink and capable of being reached for easy loading and unloading. Happily, the under-counter dishwasher automatically ensures counter space next to the sink above. However, the *dishwasher door swing should be checked* to see whether it will conflict with standing room in front of the sink or with circulation through the kitchen—a very common design problem! (Figure 2.8)

Although it is critical that the sink workstation have a view, it is equally important that it have adjacent *upper and lower cabinet storage* near the sink. Balancing these two requirements is like fine-tuning a violin; too many

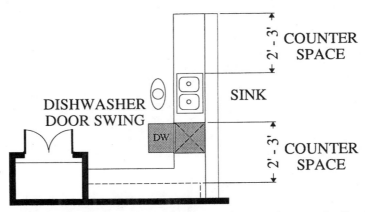

Figure 2.8 Anticipate the swing of the dishwasher door, to ensure that easy loading is feasible and that it does not interfere with circulation through the kitchen.

cabinets above the sink will block views and lead to a sense of enclosure, but locating the cabinets on a remote wall may result in an uncomfortable walk to store dishes and food. As a rule of thumb, try to have four linear feet of upper cabinets within eight feet of the sink. Likewise, try to have three linear feet of lower cabinets within six feet of the sink. (Figure 2.9)

Speaking of cabinets and storage, it's becoming more important to consider the need for adequate *waste disposal* in the kitchen. This has evolved from merely a place for the kitchen trash bin (which usually was not provided either) into a more sophisticated need to provide for disposal or storage of different classes of waste for recycling, reuse, or composting. Kitchen cabinet manufacturers have reponded to this need by introducing *waste receptacle cabinets* into their designs. These come in pull-out, swing-out and drawer varieties, with one or more bins per cabinet for separating glass, plastic, aluminum, and paper wastes. (Figure 2.9)

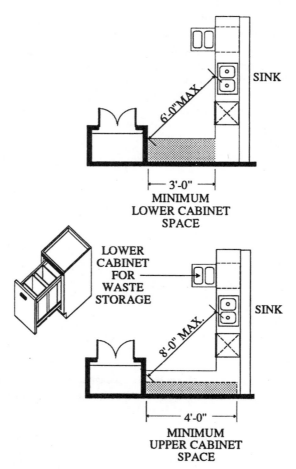

SINK

6'-0" MAX.

— 3'-0" —
MINIMUM
LOWER CABINET
SPACE

LOWER
CABINET
FOR
WASTE
STORAGE

SINK

8'-0" MAX.

— 4'-0" —
MINIMUM
UPPER CABINET
SPACE

Figure 2.9 Ample space in both upper and lower cabinets should be close to the sink. A place for wastes and recyclable storage should be included near the sink as well.

Other areas near the kitchen are also popular recycling stations, particularly if a ground floor mudroom or utility room is available. If the breakfast nook has built-in bench seating, it may be an ideal recycling center, with pull-up seats covering recycling bins (Figure 2.21). Large walk-in pantries may also be a good spot for this function.

Of growing significance in kitchen design is the fact that in the lifestyles of many types of households there is an increase in the number of cooks, all of whom often want working space at the same time. In response to this, kitchen designs now often incorporate a second sink within the kitchen, generally referred to as the *salad sink*. (Figure 2.10)

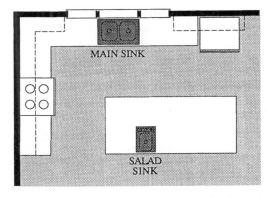

MAIN SINK

SALAD
SINK

Figure 2.10 An increasingly common feature in even modest kitchens is a second, "salad" sink, allowing two cooks to work more effectively. A separate counter and workspace is preferable for its location.

The salad sink usually has only one bowl and faucet, and needs enough adjacent counter area to permit its routine use as a secondary workstation. Whether to accommodate the grazing phenomenon or cooperative food preparation for a formal meal, this additional work area is becoming firmly established as a buyer preference, and will undoubtedly begin to appear in more and more affordable homes of the future.

The storage of food is also a vital consideration to kitchen design, and, like the role of the kitchen in the home, the philosophy of food storage is changing in response to lifestyle preferences. Increasingly, home buyers are expressing the desire to store more food for longer periods of time, a practice which reduces both the number of trips to the grocery store and the overall price of food. Extra-large refrigerators, walk-in pantries, freezers, and additional cabinet space are all used in greater frequency in response to this increasing urge to gather and store large quantities of provisions.

After the sink, the *refrigerator* is the second most important appliance. Design and layout issues here include *accessibility to and from the sink, door swing direction and clearance,* and *adjacent counter space.* Unlike the sink, the refrigerator's adjacent areas need not include shelving, but adequate counter space is vital. Two to three linear feet of counter space on the side next to the door handle will allow for loading and unloading refrigerated items. Counter space on the other side is not as important; therefore, this area can be designed for a solid wall, pantry, or other feature.

The *oven / range* is the third of the "big three" appliances found in the kitchen. Here, *adjacent shelving* is more important than counter space, but both are needed. The shelving should be accessible for pots and pans, cookware, and the other containers for meal preparation. The length of the counter next to the range can be shorter than the space devoted to sink and refrigerator areas; one to two linear feet on each side is adequate. (Figure 2.11)

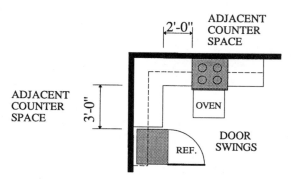

Figure 2.11 Besides providing adjacent counter space, designers should make certain that the door-swings of all appliances in the kitchen are anticipated in the overall layout.

In larger homes, the traditional oven/range appliance is generally now split into two separate appliances: the *cooktop,* and the *wall oven* or *ovens.* Further, besides the traditional gas or electric ovens, there is a separate but generally smaller *microwave oven* for warming, snacks, or preparing processed foods. Since larger homes can accommodate more kitchen space and more investment in appliances, the wall oven is viewed as a nice amenity; no longer does the cook have to stoop over to load food into the oven. The cooktop now can be placed in a more accessible location such as an island counter. Microwave ovens are likely to be used much more frequently than either the range or the cooktop, however, because of the popularity and convenience of processed foods.

The *work triangle* is a phrase commonly used to describe the circulation pattern among the three major appliances—sink, refrigerator, and oven/range. In any kitchen layout, the work triangle should be considered and even measured to ensure that the distances between the appliances are great enough to permit unimpeded preparation and cleanup activity, but not so long that distances between appliances are inconvenient. Measure the length of each leg of the triangle, then add them together. *A total length of 16 to 20 feet is optimal.* The design of many luxury kitchens violates this rule and creates unnecessary walking between workstations. (Figure 2.12)

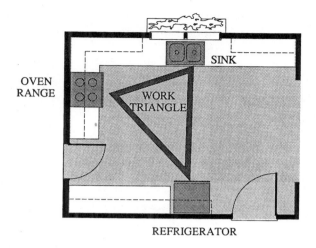

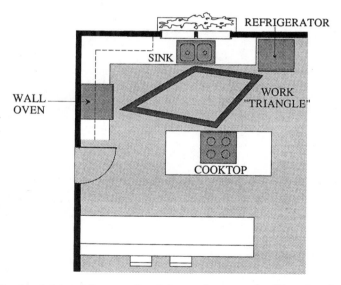

Figure 2.12 The "work triangle" among the sink, oven/range, and refrigerator should have a combined distance, or "legs," of no more than 20 feet.

Decisions regarding appliance locations often are generated from the premise that the refrigerator and the oven should be located along an *interior wall*. Because these appliances eliminate view opportunities, interior walls are preferred. An interior wall is also ideal for mounting overhead cabinets, leaving the area above the sink open for views of the outdoors or of adjacent spaces in the community component. (Figure 2.13)

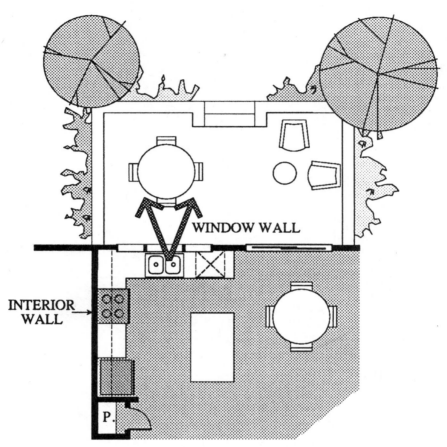

Figure 2.13 When possible, locate the oven/range, refrigerator, and pantry on interior walls, so that the sink can have a window wall with a view.

Optimal layouts for kitchen counters avoid right angles, because each corner means poor access to internal counters and shelves. For function, the *galley kitchen* configuration is most efficient, but is not the first choice of consumers because it can feel "tight" and is not conducive to socializing while cooking. Also, try to the avoid the U-shape, as this configuration includes two corners. A popular current layout includes an L-shaped counter with an adjacent island. In order to avoid lost space at the corner of the "L," a *corner pantry* may be considered. Another alternative for effective use of the corner is a *corner sink,* because the area below the sink generally is lost to plumbing anyway. (Figure 2.14)

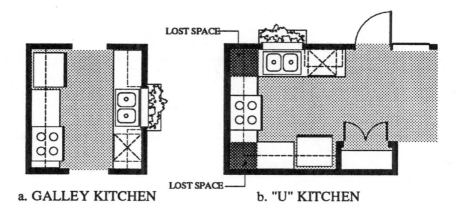

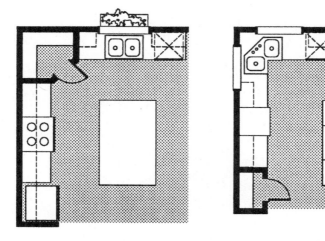

a. GALLEY KITCHEN

b. "U" KITCHEN

c. "L" KITCHEN WITH
   ISLAND AND CORNER
   PANTRY

d. "L" KITCHEN WITH
   ISLAND AND CORNER
   SINK

Figure 2.14 While efficient, "galley" kitchen plans (a) are generally unpopular with buyers; "U"-shaped counters (b) have some drawbacks as a result of the lost space that occurs in the corners. A better layout is an "L"-shaped counter with an island, using the corner as a pantry (c) or as a corner sink (d).

An *island counter* is an extremely popular feature in contemporary kitchens. When an island counter is combined with an L-shaped counter, an efficient, workable counter layout results. The island can also be utilized as a buffer between the kitchen and the breakfast/family areas, while still leaving the kitchen open and accessible to those rooms. Further, the difficult-to-reach corner can be used as a pantry or a sink, avoiding the lost space of typical corner counters.

Typically, island counters do not include overhead cabinets. A sink or cook-top can be located here, but in affordable designs, sinks create plumbing complications, and cooktops may have safety concerns. So for those markets it may be best to leave the island countertop open. For larger, move-up homes, island counter design has become the focal point of designer kitchens. Now trends include combining upper and lower-height counters for both preparing food and eating. The island counter is also used for displaying items such as books, special foods and drinks, and even media devices (the television). Island designs undoubtedly will continue to evolve in design sophistication in response to lifestyle design preferences. (Figure 2.15)

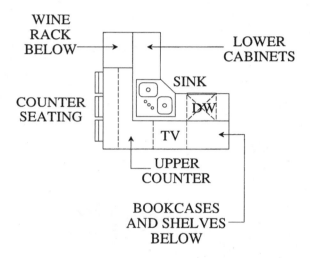

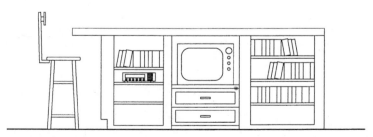

Figure 2.15 Island counters are becoming the focal point of upscale kitchens with designs calling for multifunctional uses on all sides.

In most contemporary kitchens the *pantry* is also a standard element. If overall design goals include the elimination of cabinets over the sink, a larger pantry can compensate for lost cabinet storage. Pantries are currently growing in size as well as in popularity. In many kitchens they are being offered as walk-ins, with extensive space reminiscent of the *larders* found in older homes.

Larders were small rooms off the kitchen—generally with a window but no heat—which were intended specifically for the long-term storage of food in a colder room. Fruits and vegetables, for example, would be stored in such a space instead of in a refrigerator. With today's lifestyle concerns including energy efficiency, conservation, and natural foods, a return to the larder concept makes sense. Here, larger quantities of food can be stored, reducing grocery trips and maintaining foods without refrigeration. These new larders can be designed to have cabinet-grade counters and shelves for extensive storage. (Figure 2.16)

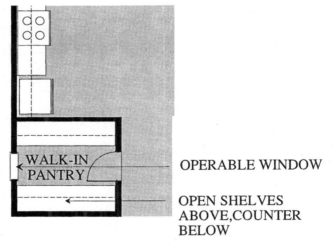

OPERABLE WINDOW

OPEN SHELVES ABOVE, COUNTER BELOW

Figure 2.16 Larger, walk-in pantries, reminiscent of the "larder" in older kitchens, are now very popular in many new homes.

Although the location of the pantry is important within the overall scheme of kitchen layout, its position is not as critical as that of the "big three" appliances. Indeed, the pantry should be outside the work triangle, since it is used for longer-term storage of foodstuffs.

A *desk* is another feature buyers are endorsing in contemporary kitchens. Properly designed and located, it can act as a workstation for supervising and tracking the many household management tasks. Like the pantry, this can be slightly off the beaten path, well outside the work triangle. The desk should be lower than normal kitchen counter height and have a work surface of four to five linear feet. A desk area may include built-in drawer space, a bulletin board, lighting, telephone, intercom, and adjacent operable windows. The design of this center should accommodate a home computer, and this area is also the logical location of the command center for housewide communication and environmental controls. (Figure 2.17) With the growing affordability and application of computers for home use, a major question of design significance is, where does the household computer belong? Let's face it, the computer is used for work, play, and learning, and needs an accessible location in the community component.

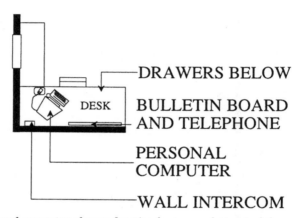

Figure 2.17 Desks and computer alcoves function best near, but out of the way of, the kitchen's work triangle.

As computers and related multimedia devices have become more prevalent in people's homes, they are being accommodated in various locations within the home, both in the community and privacy components. One solution is the centrally located *home computer station,* which can be an alcove off a highly used space such as the kitchen or family room. This is a nonterritorial space that can be used by any household member. As home computing becomes even more affordable, and in larger and more mature households, *computer lofts* off bedrooms will also offer shared spaces for the use of the computer.

After considering the kitchen layout's functional requirements, be sure to acknowledge the kitchen's role as a social center. Seating locations at the breakfast area should be readily accessible and within eye contact or earshot of kitchen workstations. It should be possible to easily carry on a conversation with someone working at the sink or adjacent counter area from adjacent rooms. Again, the benefits of an open area in front of the sink include establishing this location as a "stage" for conversing with or entertaining guests. (Figures 2.18 and 2.19)

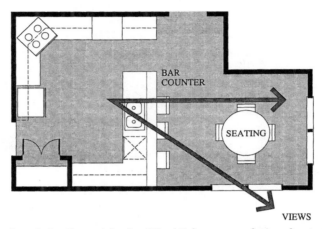

Figure 2.18 To acknowledge the social role of the kitchen, many designs locate the sink facing a seating area to permit conversation and exchange.

Figure 2.19 The view from the sink should not be blocked by overhead cabinets.

Breakfast Area

The breakfast area, or informal dining area, is part and parcel of the kitchen. The historical ancestor of the breakfast area is the country kitchen, where the dining table was right in the middle of the kitchen. Over time, floor plans have been modified to accommodate this space into separate nooks and crannies, which evolved into today's breakfast area.

The breakfast area should accommodate at least a 48-inch-diameter table

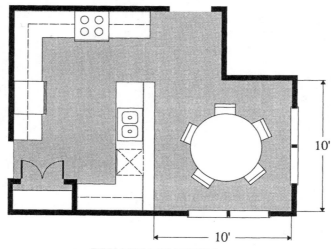

a. BREAKFAST ROOM

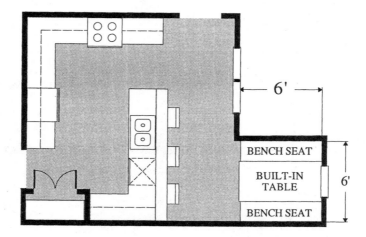

b. BREAKFAST NOOK

Figure 2.20 (*a*) The breakfast room should have realistic dimensions to accommodate a moderate-size table with seating for 4 to 6 people. (*b*) For smaller households, the cozy "nook" space is also regaining popularity as a breakfast area.

and four chairs. Typically, it is at least an 8- by 8-foot space. This size is sufficient only if there is no circulation through this space; otherwise, dimensions should increase to at least 10 by 10 feet. A recent trend in breakfast area design has been a movement back to the cozy "nook" space found in older kitchens. This smaller, built-in bench and table area can be an opportunity to create a smaller, more intimate space and is particularly attractive to smaller households (i.e., single parents, empty-nesters). Nooks offer another potential focal point for the kitchen with the built-in benches and tables often made in a quality millwork design. (Figure 2.20)

The breakfast space should also be given high priority for orientation to natural light and views; and despite the fact that this area will be used at various times, morning light should be given the highest priority. Windows, skylights, or patio doors are all good sources of natural light; if possible, locate them so that they can provide maximum sunlight throughout the day. Careful design will also extend this light to the adjoining kitchen, particularly the sink workstation. (Figure 2.21)

VIEW

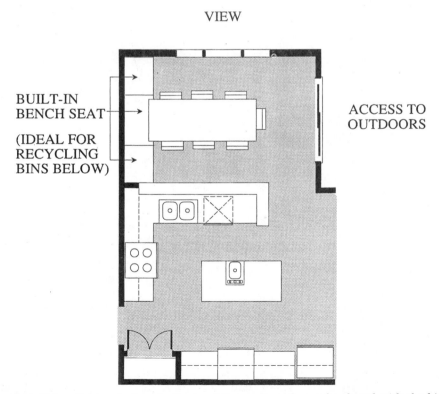

BUILT-IN
BENCH SEAT

(IDEAL FOR
RECYCLING
BINS BELOW)

ACCESS TO
OUTDOORS

Figure 2.21 Prime light and views in the breakfast area easily can be shared with the kitchen space. A built-in bench seat along one wall of the breakfast area can help make the room unique and is ideal for storing recyclables.

Direct access to the outdoor deck/patio is also a popular design feature of breakfast areas. Although French doors are more aesthetically pleasing, sliding glass doors may be functionally preferable as they have no impeding door swing. Direct access from the kitchen to the outdoor dining area is also popular. Locating a door at the heart of the kitchen work triangle will allow for easy transport of food to the outdoor table. If this is not possible, consider a pass-through window near the sink or over another counter. (Figure 2.22)

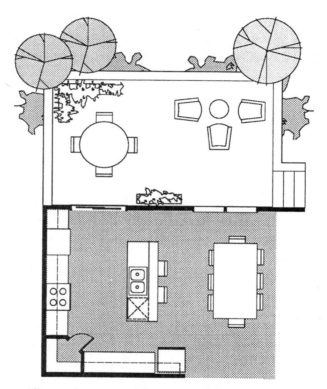

Figure 2.22 By providing outdoor access right next to kitchen counters, food can handily be delivered to an outdoor dining area—without having to circulate through the breakfast area.

Family or Living Room

The third and final element of the community component is the living or family room. In smaller homes, the family room may double as the living room and be called a "great room." Under either name, this is the place where household members can gather in a relaxed manner to share time together.

The separate family room is evolving into what may also be called a *media room*. Regardless of one's views about the positive or negative effects of the media, one cannot deny that television and its related expansive devices are immensely important elements in most households. In the age of telecommunications, designers must ensure that room configurations will provide for wide screens without letting them dominate the room. Therefore, it is wise to locate enough space for a large cabinet, or *home entertainment center*, along one wall of the family room. (Figure 2.23)

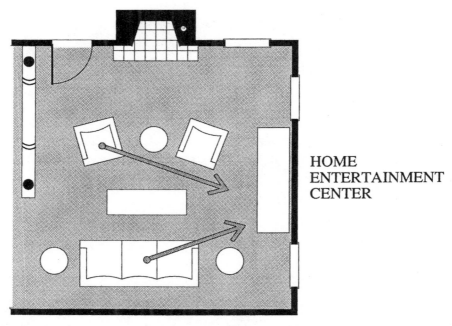

HOME
ENTERTAINMENT
CENTER

Figure 2.23 A major consideration in sizing the main living room or separate family room is to provide a location for media devices that will be accessible but will not dominate the room.

The television is, in fact, only one element of the evolving *media center*. Many separate family room designs provide a "media wall" of built-in cabinets that also hold stereo equipment, storage for tapes, videos, compact discs, and a video cassette recorder. With the popularity of home videos, and other video entertainment, the family room is now often a *defacto* in-home movie theater, which is another reason to make this area accessible to the home snack bar (the kitchen). (Figure 2.24*a*)

Another solution to the television/media center issue is the emergence of "home theaters" as separate rooms specifically for audio-visual experiences. These *media rooms* are much like dens; the idea is to get the viewing appliances out of the main living areas to achieve better noise isolation. Media rooms have proven very popular with buyers in the higher price ranges of new homes. It is expected that they will become standard rooms in even small houses in the near future. (Figure 2.24*b*)

A *fireplace* is also generally an integral element of the family room.

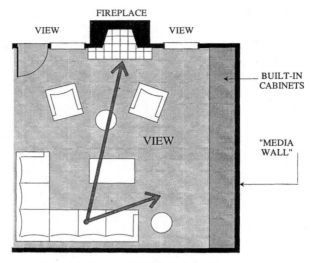

a. FAMILY ROOM WITH MEDIA WALL

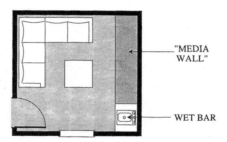

b. SEPARATE MEDIA ROOM
OR HOME THEATER

Figure 2.24 (*a*) In larger homes, the television, stereo, video recorder, and other equipment can be incorporated into a "media wall" of cabinets—with plenty of shelves for storage. From the anticipated seating area, good views of both the media wall, the outdoors, and the fireplace are all desirable. (*b*) Homes that are still larger may include a separate room for media devices, known as a "home theater."

Although households seldom use the fireplace, this amenity is important symbolically, retaining a vestigial role as the true "hearth" and the focal point for intimate gatherings. Surveys indicate that buyers would rather have the fireplace in the family room than in any other room in the house. In homes with both family room fireplaces and media walls/media centers, a key design task is to accommodate both these focal points without compromising either. This often means keeping them on opposing walls, both of which are visible from the seating area. (Figure 2.24*a*)

Prefabricated fireplaces, as opposed to historical masonry fireplaces, have become more common in production houses. The market acceptance of these less costly prefabricated models allows designers more freedom to place them in a location other than an outside wall. A very popular alternative, for example, is the two- or three-sided fireplace, which can act as a room divider and allow the fire to be viewed from several rooms. In larger homes, it is now common to have two or three fireplaces in locations such as the kitchen, master bedroom, and den areas, as well as in the family room.

In addition to the television/media wall and fireplace, the family room must also accommodate group seating with a view of both the media center and fireplace. Furnishing plans may include an L-shaped sectional couch or a sofa with two or three side chairs; the layout should also allow for a coffee table and side tables. If the design program calls for a *wet bar* or separate small sink and food/drink storage, surveys have indicated this is best located in the family room.

Because of the activity in the community component, the space flow between the three areas that form it is extremely important. People in the conversation area should be able to view both the television and the fireplace. They should also enjoy outdoor views, have easy access to the outdoors, and have the ability to converse with people in the kitchen or breakfast area.

Direct access to the outdoors from the family room through sliding glass or French doors is almost universally popular. In temperate climates, a well-appointed outdoor deck is an extension of not only the family area but the entire community component. In some markets, the deck or patio should be accessible from almost every room of the house. An example is the south Florida pool/lanai, easily reached from virtually all rooms in the home; another is the hacienda plan of the Southwest or the courtyard houses of California. A deck/patio area is desirable in any climate, as discussed further in Chapter 6. (Figure 2.25)

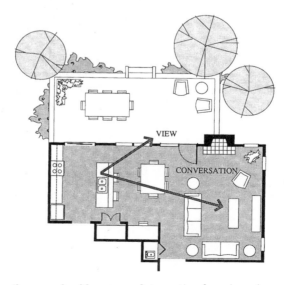

Figure 2.25 The family room should accommodate seating for prime views, easy access to the outdoors, and conversation with people in the kitchen, as well as separate activity areas.

The family room and the entire community component is often a popular location for volume ceilings, specialty windows, and balcony overlooks, but the design drama these elements create will probably be more desirable to younger and/or nontraditional buyers. Generally, conservative buyers may prefer the more intimate environments created by modest ceiling heights. The introduction of volume to the family room is probably more acceptable to buyers with traditional preferences if the overall floor plan is small and in need of visual expansion. (Figure 2.26)

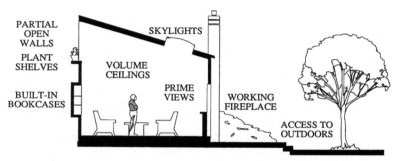

Figure 2.26 The family room is a very popular location for features such as volume space, along with skylights, bookcases, a fireplace, plant shelves, and easy outdoor access.

Recent buyer surveys have shown that people seem to a have a growing preference for a triangular relationship between the kitchen, breakfast room, and family room. This makes sense, because it pulls these three spaces closer together for ease of function and conversation. A typical plan solution is to pull one of the three spaces "out of the envelope" so that a triangular relationship will result. This also gives the protruded room additional light and view access. (Figure 2.27)

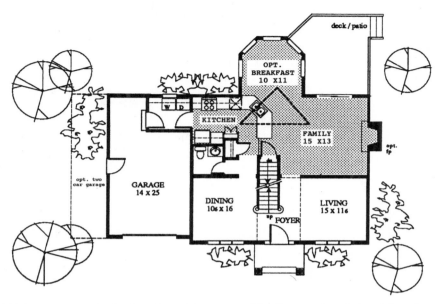

Figure 2.27 Arranging the kitchen, breakfast area, and family room in a "triangle" configuration makes sense; it pulls the community component elements together for improved conversation.

The other major trend in room relationships within the community component is the movement toward developing *niches* or *alcoves* for different functions (such as the computer center discussed earlier) off the common spaces. This favors small protrusions in the plan for tables, desks, and seating, where people can perform individual functions while remaining within earshot of the larger group.

The kitchen, breakfast, and family rooms form the community component. This is the "common ground" within the home's living quarters. It is distinguished by heavy use and by its importance as the meeting place for everyday life. Complementing the community area is the privacy component. This is where people retreat to their individual environments, so these spaces also need significant design attention if they are to function properly.

3

The Privacy Component: Master Suite, Secondary Bedroom Block, Guest Suite, and Den/Library

Everyone needs to be able to strike a balance between community and privacy. Just as we want to be together with family and friends, we also feel the alternate desire to be alone for creative pursuits, for study, reading, and reflective thought. The areas of the home designed for this is known as the *privacy component*. (Figure 3.1)

Historically, the locations for privacy in most homes have been the bedrooms. Here, individuals retreat at the end of their daily routine to prepare themselves for yet another day. This may include homework for children or reading for adults. Watching the late-night news before retiring has also become an evening ritual in many American homes.

Thirty years ago all bedrooms were usually located on the second floor of the house right next to one another. The *master bedroom* and *secondary bedrooms* were close to each other and similar in size, with little but a private bathroom to distinguish the master bedroom from the other bedrooms (Figure 3.2). Contemporary homes, on the other hand, address the need for privacy between different bedrooms. Current plans generally separate parents, chil-

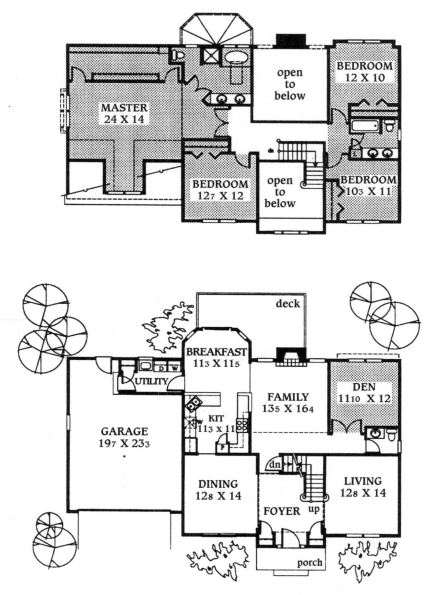

Figure 3.1 The privacy component typically includes bedrooms, dens, libraries, home offices, guest suites, and other rooms used for quiet retreat.

dren, and guests into zones that are remote from one another for maximum privacy.

In two-story homes, the preference for designs with a master suite on the first floor has increased. This allows the secondary bedrooms to occupy upper-floor space, separated both vertically and horizontally from the master bedroom. In ranch-style homes, the master suite and secondary bedroom block

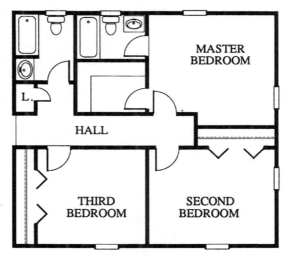

Figure 3.2 In older homes, all bedrooms were in relatively similar sizes and were located close to each other.

often form "wings" on opposite sides of the house. (Figure 3.3) Both solutions pull these bedrooms apart to achieve some distance between heads of household and children, or between owners and guests. This type of separation is desirable for many household profiles, with the possible exception of parents with babies and very young children, who may prefer a closer connection between the master and secondary bedrooms.

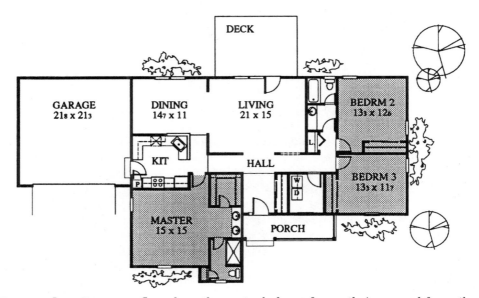

Figure 3.3 In contemporary floor plans, the master bedroom frequently is removed from other bedrooms to form remote "bedroom wings" for maximum privacy.

In larger homes, the *guest suite* may be a third element of the privacy component. In modest, move-up homes, the guest suite can also serve as a *den/library*. In even larger homes, guest quarters may comprise a separate, self-contained wing; when not in use by visitors, this area is ideal as a private space that household members can enjoy for a variety of quiet activities, or as the much-needed *home office*. (Figure 3.4)

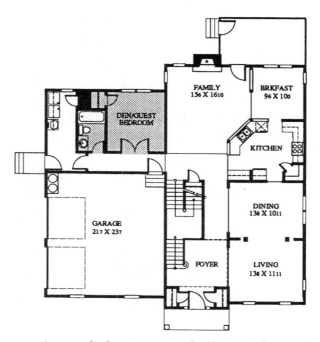

Figure 3.4   A guest suite may also be a separate and self-contained wing. When not in use by visitors, the room can double as a den or library.

The trend toward *multiple master suites* within a larger home is part of this third element of the privacy component. In today's households, the need to accommodate individuals such as children home from college, older family members, or temporary live-in help, calls for a more self-contained space within the privacy component. This may include a mini-kitchen and/or a separate entrance, among other features.

When designed as separate or semiprivate quarters, the guest-suite wing offers options that address the lifestyle and preferences of a variety of market groups. For homeowners whose parents or in-laws make extended visits or move into the home permanently, the guest-wing design delivers the privacy that all parties appreciate. Live-ins, such as *au pairs,* gain a beneficial degree of autonomy at day's end. The guest suite can also be converted to a home-office space at some point.

Reviewing the design requirements of the privacy component involves a detailed analysis of each part, and should start with the master suite, long identified as being the most important area of the home as the domain of the owners. Unlike the kitchen, where function is the final arbiter of the design, the master-suite design must respond to strong emotional issues.

Master Suite

The master suite's role within a contemporary home is as an isolated retreat. Although we generally think of the master suite as having two spaces—the bedroom and the bathroom—the ideal configuration of a well-defined master suite actually has five distinct areas: *sleeping, sitting, dressing, closet,* and *bath*. These are best-located to each other with a circulation triangle (similar to the kitchen work triangle) between the sitting, sleeping, and dressing areas. (Figure 3.5)

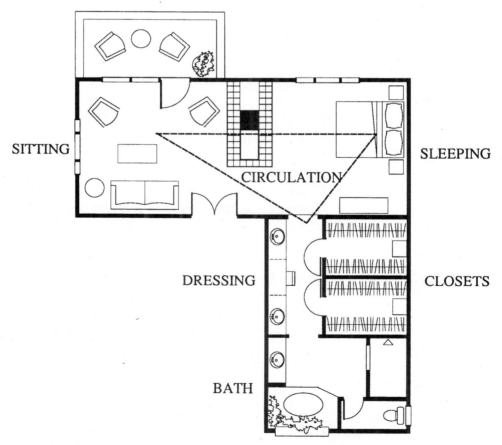

Figure 3.5 The master suite includes five distinct areas. A circulation triangle between the sitting, sleeping, and dressing areas is optimal.

Sleeping area

Of the five areas in the master suite, the most hours are spent in the *sleeping area,* but its location may be subordinated, for view considerations, to the *sitting area.* The sleeping area may be one area of the home where dark, internalized space is an asset. It should accommodate a king-size bed with 30 inches of clearance around the perimeter. The room should be designed to accommodate a bed on at least one wall, with an option for an alternate location if possible. If the *bed wall* is an exterior wall, there should be no windows on walls where the bed is likely to go. Besides being aesthetically undesirable, a window blocked by the headboard of a bed is also unreachable for operation, which diminishes comfort and privacy. (Figure 3.6)

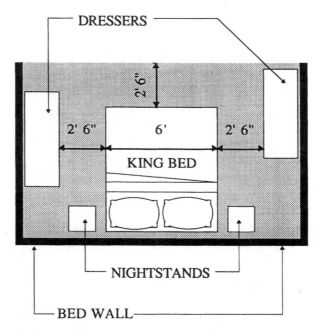

Figure 3.6 The sleeping area should accommodate a king-size bed, with 30 inches of clearance on three sides. It should also have room for nightstands on either side and two dressers nearby.

If the bed is to be located along an interior wall (which is generally preferable), the use of the adjoining room must be considered. As with any bedroom, the master suite should not share common walls with such active, noisy rooms as the laundry or a secondary bath.

Although the bed is the major furnishing to be accommodated in the sleeping area, additional standard items to consider when dimensions are established include *two night stands,* one at each side of the bed, and *two dressers.* A location for a media cabinet (for a television) should also be anticipated—one that accommodates viewing both from a reclining position in the bed and from the sitting area. (Figure 3.7)

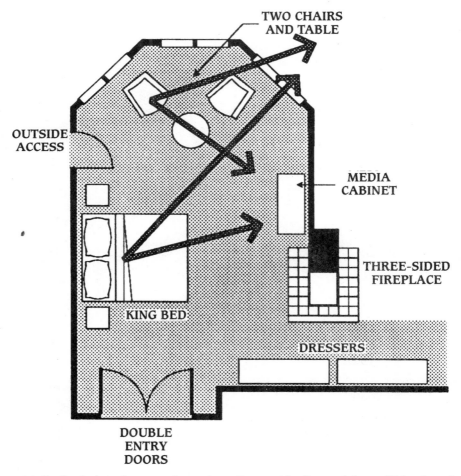

Figure 3.7 In the design of an upscale master suite, consider the need for multiple views from both sitting and sleeping areas. Other popular amenities include direct outdoor access, a fireplace, and double entry doors.

Sitting area

The *sitting area* is the other space the designer should provide for in the master suite's bedroom area. Even when it is seldom used, a sitting area adds graciousness to the entire suite. In smaller master suites, the sitting area may simply be a location for *two chairs,* whereas in large suites, the sitting area should accommodate at least *several chairs, a desk,* and possibly *a sofa* for reading, relaxing, or conversing. (Figure 3.8)

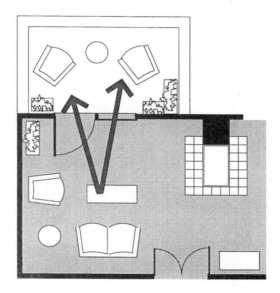

SEPARATE SITTING ROOM

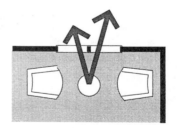

SMALL SITTING
AREA

Figure 3.8 Sitting areas may be very small, with just enough room for one or two chairs and a table. In other cases, it can be a well-defined room with space for a sofa and fireplace.

The sitting area should have a prime location near windows for views, access to a balcony or patio, and possibly a fireplace. Natural light is very desirable here, and since pleasant vistas will most often be enjoyed while one is sitting or lounging, *lower sills* on these windows provide for more enjoyment. (Figure 3.9)

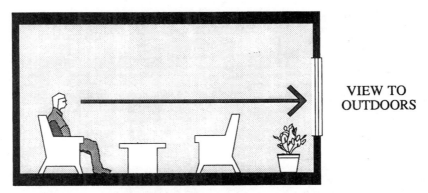

Figure 3.9 Window heights in sitting areas should allow for views from the seated position.

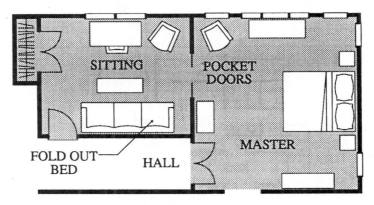

Figure 3.10 The sitting room can double as an extra bedroom with doors to both the hall and the master bedroom. This type of flexible room can evolve from a nursery, to a guest room, to a home office over a period of time in the homeowners' life.

In some cases, the master suite may be designed with a sitting room that could also function as a separate *library* or *guest bedroom*. If this room has direct access to both the master suite and the hall, the buyer can easily exercise this option before or after the purchase (Figure 3.10). This type of flexible room can evolve from a nursery to a sitting room, to a guest room, or to a home office, depending on the owners' changing lifestyle over a period of time.

Sitting alcoves can be separated from the sleeping area by discreet room dividers. Two-sided fireplaces are increasingly popular, along with partial-height walls, planters, and steps. Changes in the ceiling height or wall materials can further define the sitting area. An immediate view of the sitting area upon entry into the master suite will help make an attractive first impression of the suite; the initial view may include a picturesque balcony or fireplace as well. Alternatively, the entry into the master suite should keep the sleeping area and bed out of sight. (Figure 3.11)

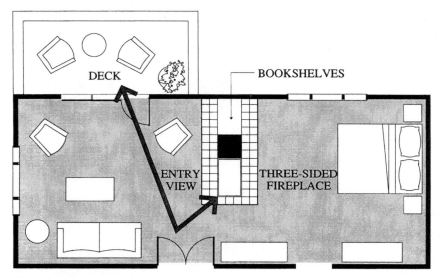

Figure 3.11 The sitting area may be partially separated from the sleeping area by a special divider such as a three-sided fireplace. The initial view upon entry into an upscale master suite should be impressive and should avoid immediate view of the sleeping area and bed.

Closet

Tucked away from the rest of the suite, but of critical importance, are the *closets*. Small or poorly planned closets in the master suite can be the kiss of death for new-home sales. If closets do not correspond to the spacious dimensions of a large master suite, they can make the entire suite—and house— seem poorly designed and may even make it unsalable.

In the master suite, *walk-in closets* are preferred, hands down. Linear closets should be used in smaller houses only if square footage is truly at a premium. In larger houses separate "his" and "her" closets are highly popular, reflecting the natural desire of people for their own private space. Closet dimensions should reflect the ideal configuration for storing clothes. Here, *rod and shelf length* is the measure of performance. Probably the optimal shape for a walk-in closet is a rectangle, with rods and shelves on both sides and circulation down the middle. The addition of a third perpendicular rod and shelf at the back of the closet often may look good on paper but, in reality, may not produce much additional clothes storage. With this closet configuration, the door should swing *out,* so that it won't block any of the interior rods or shelves when it is open. (Figure 3.12)

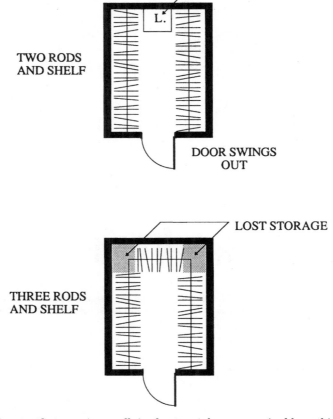

Figure 3.12 The use of corners in a walk-in closet may be compromised by a third rod and shelf. Try to locate a linen closet on the center wall instead.

The minimum width of a double-loaded walk-in closet should be 6 feet. This allows for a 2-foot-deep shelf along both sides, with a minimum 2-foot aisle between. Wishful thinking on paper may seek to reduce this, but a reduction will create cramped accessibility. If the six-foot width cannot be achieved, an *L-shaped* rod-and-shelf configuration is the next most desirable. In this case, the door can swing in toward the closet's interior blank wall. (Figure 3.13)

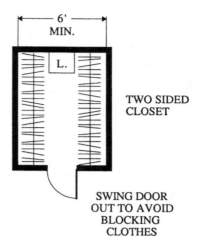

TWO SIDED
CLOSET

SWING DOOR
OUT TO AVOID
BLOCKING
CLOTHES

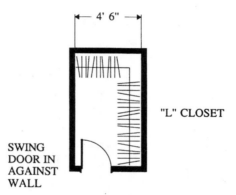

"L" CLOSET

SWING
DOOR IN
AGAINST
WALL

Figure 3.13 A six-foot width usually is the minimum for accommodating rods and shelves on either side of the closet. Smaller widths should have "L"-shaped rods and shelves.

Dressing area

Adjacent to the closet and the bath, but slightly out of view from the rest of the suite, is the *dressing area*. This is the locale for grooming and selecting and donning clothing before meeting the world.

The focus of the dressing area is the *vanity*. The vanity may include one or two washbowls, along with an integral place to sit. A *large mirror* should be located above the vanity, and the entire space should incorporate *generous lighting*. Natural light is very popular in the dressing area, with skylights as a common option. For average-size houses, vanity lengths of 5 to 6 feet are desirable. A shorter vanity should include only one washbowl, as two will reduce valuable counter space. To accommodate two washbowls and seating, the vanity should be 8 to 12 linear feet. Drawers below and medicine cabinets at either side wall of the vanity will provide for necessary storage of toiletries. (Figure 3.14)

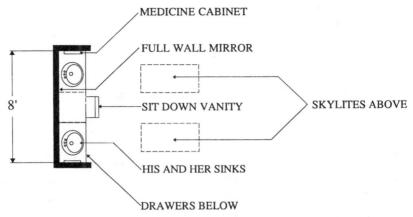

Figure 3.14 The dressing area often features a premium vanity with two sinks and a seating area in the center.

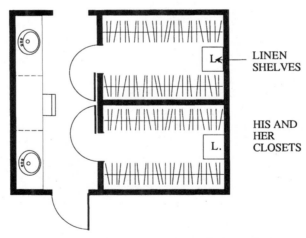

Figure 3.15 Behind the vanity is the ideal location for closets. In larger homes, separate "his" and "her" closets are also popular.

The dressing area should also have a generous *linen closet,* either beside the vanity or along a wall near the closet. In smaller homes, the linen closet may be located within the closet itself and simply consist of a series of open shelves. In larger homes, *separate linen closets* for each person are emerging as a popular feature in the master suite. In either case, linen closets should be adequately sized, with 2 foot by 2 foot as a minimum shelf size, usually spaced at least a foot apart vertically. (Figure 3.15)

Bath area

In design significance, the *master bath* in contemporary homes is on a par with the kitchen. As with the kitchen, function is important, but *drama* and the *desire for luxury* are even more significant, particularly in large houses. The master bath is often the centerpiece or a focal point of a master suite bathroom.

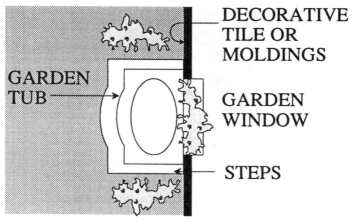

Figure 3.16 The garden tub may be elevated or sunken, with windows above and quality finishes surrounding it.

Current design emphasis on the master bath can be attributed to a variety of trends, including an increased concern for physical health and well-being. For centuries, public bathing was regarded as a healthy and uplifting process—reflected in the great public baths of the Roman Empire and in contemporary communal baths in Japan and Europe. One sees these values in today's public health spas, and in the home, with the popular *garden tub* in the master bathroom.

Indeed, the *garden tub* is usually the focal point of the entire master bath. Often sunken or elevated, the tub has become a domestic icon, framed with accent walls of decorative tile and illuminated by adjacent windows. It may also be a *spa tub* which includes water jets to create a whirlpool effect. (Figure 3.16)

Although the *shower* probably will be used as the facility for daily washing, the tub is more desirable for soaking and relaxing, for daydreaming, and for the fantasy or reality of a romantic *tête-à-tête*.

Although in smaller bathrooms the garden tub must double as a shower, a common alternative is to separate the shower by building a *shower enclosure*.

Generally the shower is used daily, and its design has evolved away from the standard 3- by 3-foot bay, with shower stalls increased to 4 by 6 feet or larger, with generous glass doors, and low curb steps for easy access. Elaborate prefabricated shower designs are coming equipped with multiple spray jets for a shower/massage effect. These are quite popular with upscale buyers. Within the bath, the garden tub generally is given locational preference as a display item. The shower, on the other hand, needs only a functional location. (Figure 3.17)

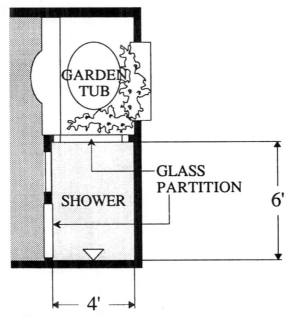

Figure 3.17 A large walk-in shower may be separated from the garden tub by a glass partition allowing light into the shower.

The third essential item in the master bath is the *toilet*. Although the garden tub is the centerpiece and the shower can easily be left on display, the toilet should be discreetly tucked away from view. If space permits, placing the toilet in a separate compartment or room provides for total privacy—a concept preferred by more than half of all buyers.

If the toilet cannot be in a separate compartment, it should at least be screened by partial-height walls in a remote location within the bath, away from the entry view. (Figure 3.18a) If compartmentalization is possible, care should be taken to avoid making the enclosure claustrophobic. Here, a small window for ventilation may be one of the home's most appreciated openings.

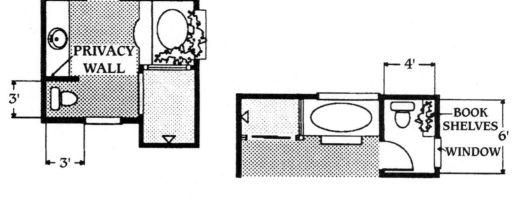

a. PRIVACY WALL   b. ENCLOSED TOILET ROOM

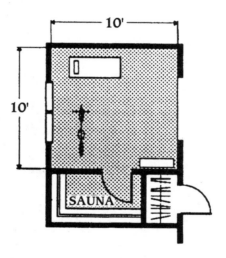

c. SMALL EXERCISE ROOM

Figure 3.18 While a compartmentalized toilet is preferred (*b*), a discreet location is always necessary (*a*). An exercise area off the master dressing area is also an increasingly popular feature for upscale homes (*c*).

This room may also have *small shelves* for plants or a *reading rack* for magazines. It could therefore appropriately be called "the reading room." (Figure 3.18*b*) In larger homes, including a *bidet* next to the toilet is also recommended, as it will become more of a standard feature in new move-up homes.

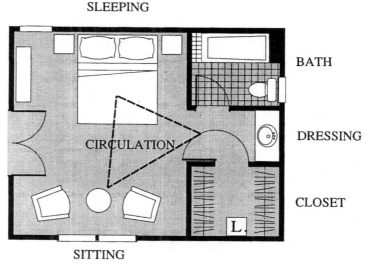

SLEEPING

BATH

DRESSING

CLOSET

CIRCULATION

SITTING

Figure 3.19 Even a small space can accommodate the five principal areas of the master suite.

Another space within the master suite that is becoming increasingly popular is an *exercise area.* This space is generally close to the dressing and bath area, and includes lots of natural light, but ideally is screened from the elegant sitting and sleeping areas. It should be able to accommodate one or more pieces of exercise equipment such as a rowing machine, stationary bicycle, or treadmill. It may also include the popular home *sauna* as a built-in feature. (Figure 3.18c)

The distinction between the bath and dressing areas may blur depending on regional lifestyle preferences. For example, in sunbelt markets, the bath and dressing areas often blend into one large space, whereas in northern, more traditional markets, the preference for differentiation between the bath and dressing areas is still quite strong. In either case, at least the toilet should be closed off in some fashion from the rest of the suite.

With careful planning, even small homes can include all five areas of the master suite. To combine these five elements into a functional layout, an optimal arrangement aligns the *bath, dressing room,* and *closet* on one side of the room. In concert with the sitting and sleeping area, these three areas as a whole then establish a *circulation triangle.* (Figure 3.19) As with other components of a home, efficient circulation is of primary concern. Poor planning generates awkward layouts and circulation problems that commonly include:

1. Having to walk through the bath to get to the closet. (Figure 3.20*a*)
2. Having to travel from the bath through the entire suite to reach the closet. (Figure 3.20*b*)
3. Having to enter the suite and walk by the bath and/or closet to get to the rest of the suite. (Figure 3.20*c*)

In most cases, a reconfiguration of the master suite areas can effectively accommodate the above-mentioned five spaces without adding additional square footage. Careful consideration of sensible furniture layouts will also help create a functional and livable master suite.

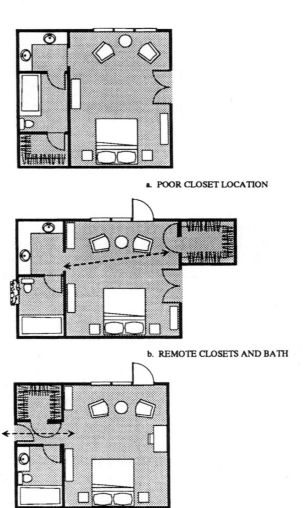

a. POOR CLOSET LOCATION

b. REMOTE CLOSETS AND BATH

c. POOR ENTRY SEQUENCE

Figure 3.20 Common problems in master suite layouts include (*a*) having to go through the bath to get to the closet, (*b*) a remote relationship between the bath and closet, and (*c*) having to walk past the bath to get to the rest of the suite.

Secondary Bedroom Block

Apart from the master suite is the other major element of the privacy component, the *secondary bedroom block.* This generally includes *two to three extra bedrooms,* at least *one full bath, a hallway,* and sometimes a *loft/overlook space* if the secondary bedrooms are upstairs. The secondary bedroom block is the domain of children, live-ins, other relatives, and occasional guests.

The organization of the secondary bedroom block should include *discreet bath access* as a primary concern. Occupants of any of the bedrooms should be able to walk from the bedroom to the bath in private, without having to travel an excessive distance. An *enclosed hallway* that connects these bedrooms to the bath helps to promote this necessary privacy. (Figure 3.21)

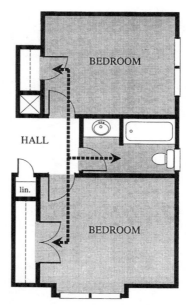

Figure 3.21 Discreet access to the secondary bath from the secondary bedrooms is a key design objective; another objective is minimizing the circulation between the entry door and the closet.

Second bathroom

Despite the fact that the second bath is very heavily used, its design is generally considered much less significant than the master bath's. However, progressive new floor plans devote a more gracious space to the secondary bath, which historically has been plugged into a 5- by 8-foot rectangular bay, just enough to allow for a minimal vanity, toilet, and tub. The secondary bath, however, is one room where investing a few additional inches will make a noticeable and favorable difference.

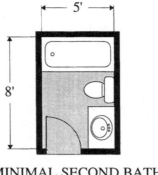

MINIMAL SECOND BATH

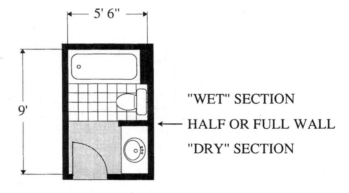

"WET" SECTION

HALF OR FULL WALL

"DRY" SECTION

UPGRADED SECOND BATH

Figure 3.22 Investing a few more inches into a minimal second bath can allow some much-needed space. A definition between "wet" and "dry" areas is also appreciated in some markets.

A more comfortable 5½- by 9-foot bath can allow for *compartmentalization* between the *toilet/tub* area and the *vanity/dressing* area, forming a clean break between "wet" and "dry" activities. If compartments would be claustrophobic, a simple half-wall between them will screen the toilet/tub area and create a feeling of separation without being closed in. (Figure 3.22)

In larger houses the vanity in the second bath ideally is 4 to 6 feet long. *Two washbowls* may or may not be desirable, depending on the lifestyle preferences, but the vanity area should always include *good lighting, a full-length mirror, a medicine cabinet,* and *undercounter storage.* (Figure 3.23)

Locating a window in the second bath often creates a dilemma. Generally, the vanity, toilet, and tub are lined up along an interior plumbing wall, which leaves only the outside wall of the tub available for a window. This is less than ideal, because of privacy, access, and water protection issues. An alternate configuration rotates the tub/toilet so that a *window* can be located over the toilet, easily accessible for operation. If the bath has other exterior walls, there might be a better window placement. (Figure 3.24)

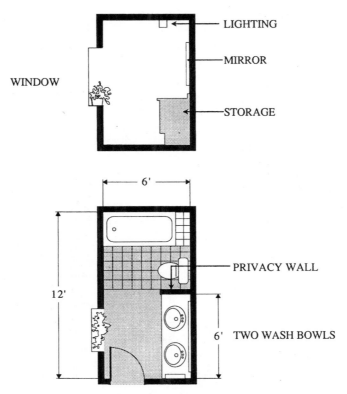

Figure 3.23 Larger homes may have secondary baths with double-bowl vanities, garden windows, and deeper tubs. Good lighting, a full-length mirror, accessible medicine cabinets, and under-counter storage are also important.

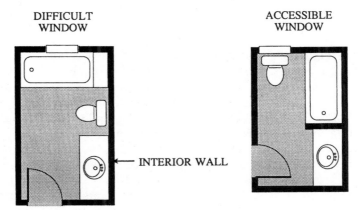

Figure 3.24 Locating the tub along an outside wall creates a problem; it's difficult to locate a window there. It's better.to locate the tub along an interior wall to allow placement of a more accessible window to the outside.

The second bath should always include a *linen closet,* located either inside the bath area or in the adjacent hallway. (Consumers have indicated they prefer that the closet be *in* the bath.) The linen closet's interior dimensions should be no less than 2 by 2 feet, forming a vertical shaft with plenty of shelves. As a minimum, an 18-inch-wide door is adequate, but 24 inches is more desirable. (Figure 3.25)

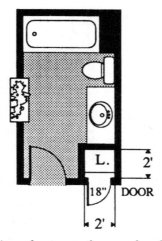

Figure 3.25 A two-foot-square linen closet near the secondary bath is a necessary storage area often overlooked.

Secondary bedrooms

Configuring the actual bedrooms of the bedroom block is relatively straightforward. Start the layout with an *entry door* near the hall bath and *locate the bedroom closet as close to the entry as possible.* Avoid *cross-circulation* through the room to reach the closet; it decreases flexibility for furniture layouts.

The location of secondary bedrooms should also consider *the noise potential of adjacent rooms.* Common walls with other bedrooms or plumbing walls should be avoided. Both closets and baths can be used as buffers between adjacent bedrooms, muffling, if not eliminating, unwanted noise. (Figure 3.26)

Bedroom window locations should not intrude into *furniture walls* for the main item of furniture—*the bed.* For that reason, windows may punctuate walls near the corners of the room rather than the center of a wall. Grouping two windows at an exterior corner is an especially pleasing solution and can expand the view from the room. However, windows located in opposite corners of the room will allow for better cross-ventilation. (Figure 3.27)

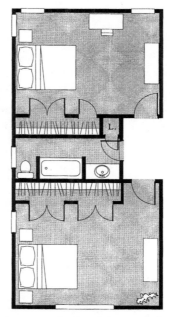

Figure 3.26 Closets can be used as noise buffers between bedrooms, or between bedrooms and bathrooms. Also, closets should be located so that they are near the entry door to minimize cross-circulation.

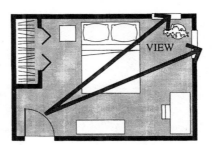

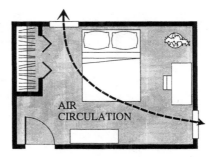

Figure 3.27 Corner windows in bedrooms may have better visual impact, but remote windows offer better ventilation.

SMALL WALK-IN CLOSET

LINEAR CLOSET

Figure 3.28 Linear closets are more acceptable in secondary bedrooms. In upscale markets, swing doors are more popular than bifolds or bypass doors. Small walk-in closets are also very popular where space allows.

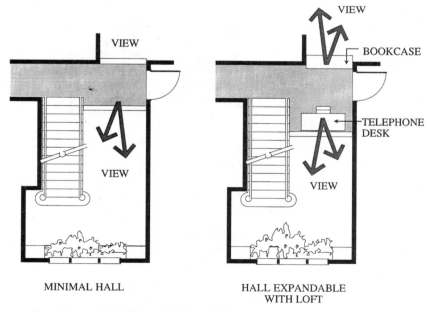

MINIMAL HALL

HALL EXPANDABLE
WITH LOFT

Figure 3.29 By adding a few feet to the width of a hallway, space for a small piece of furniture or a bookcase can make a circulation space more useful.

Linear closets are much more acceptable in the secondary bedrooms than in the master suite, but if space permits, *small walk-ins are again preferable* to linear closets. In response to consumer preferences, a pair of conventional *swing doors* are generally replacing *bifolds* or *sliders* for linear closets, particularly in larger houses. (Figure 3.28)

Hall/Loft area

Generally viewed as mere circulation, the *hall area* of the privacy component can be far more useful. Slightly expanded dimensions can allow for accessory furniture such as a telephone desk, bookcases, chairs, or other specialty furniture items. When the secondary bedrooms are on the upper level, the hall can incorporate a dramatic overlook to the first floor. (Figure 3.29)

A common extension of the upper hall is the open *loft/sitting area.* A loft may incorporate space that for various reasons was unacceptable as a bedroom; it may be too small, or may not have windows, for example. The loft space may be combined with the hall area to form an open *sitting area/study* for common use. Keeping this area open to volume spaces below is a popular option.

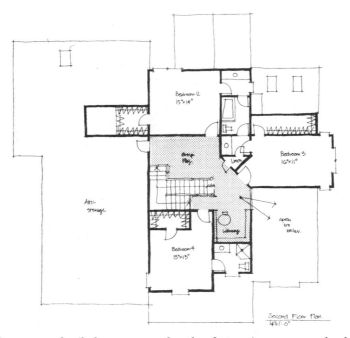

Figure 3.30 In move-up family homes, a popular plan feature is a common play loft where children can engage in joint activities.

In move-up family homes, designs that include common *play lofts* where children can engage in joint activities, are very popular. A play loft should be programmed like a small bedroom, with places for desks, shelves, and lots of natural light. Play lofts, open libraries, and second floor "free space" are best designed with several alcoves, with places for games, bookshelves, and desks that may accommodate upstairs shared computers. (Figure 3.30)

Guest Suite/Library

In larger, move-up homes, the *guest suite* may add a third element to the privacy component. Ideally, it will be separated from both the master suite *and* the secondary bedroom block, carving out another location within the house for the privacy component. A common location for the guest suite is on the first floor near the powder room, where it can double as a *library/den*. This allows for a position isolated from the other rooms in the home, yet affording easy access for its other function as a *library/den.*

The design requirements of a typical bedroom should be reinforced if the *guest suite/library/den* is to be truly functional and welcoming for overnight visitors. Providing a closet and discreet or direct access to the bath/powder room is desirable, as is a layout that allows for a *sofa bed,* workable for both day and night use. When this room is used as a guest room, the powder room can be as a full bath and may even include its own linen closet. (Figure 3.31)

To fulfill its dual role as a library/den, the guest suite may have two doors— one a set of ceremonial double doors (when it acts as a den) and a second private-access door to the hall/bath (when it is used as a guest suite). In still larger move-up houses, the *guest suite* may be a wing in and of itself, with no need to double as a library/den. In this case, the guest suite should be in a remote location; over the garage on the second floor, for example, is an increasingly popular site. With this type of guest suite (or retreat), the size requirements

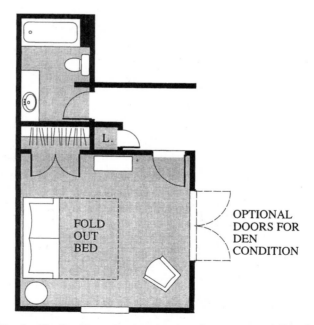

Figure 3.31 The guest suite should offer discreet access to a powder room or a full bath. Designs may include optional double doors, to allow the room to function as a den.

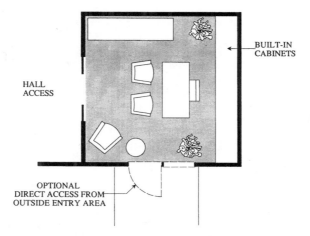

HALL
ACCESS

BUILT-IN
CABINETS

OPTIONAL
DIRECT ACCESS FROM
OUTSIDE ENTRY AREA

Figure 3.32 A library/den or home office should be designed to primarily accommodate reading and work areas with lots of shelves and room for desks and chairs. Direct access from the hall, and even the outside entry area, is desirable.

for the bedroom and bath fall somewhere between the master and the secondary bedroom block, depending on the size and price of the house.

Home Office

If a home includes a true guest suite, it will generally be large enough to have a *true library/den* as well. The role of this type of room is both public and private, accessible to the balance of the home yet secluded enough to provide a feeling of retreat. The library/den may function as the *home office* as well.

The *true library/den* generally is located on the first floor near the entry or living room. This room is one of the few spaces in the house that does not need much natural light. More important is the need for *wall space* to accommodate *bookshelves, cabinets,* and *storage areas.* Because light and views usually are not an issue, the library is one room that can be located internally on the lot. Sound isolation, however, should be reviewed, with common walls located for minimal noise.

If the den is likely to be used as a home office, a location off the entry hall is desirable. It may even be wise to include a direct outdoor-access door (such as French doors) to an entry court patio, as business visitors may feel more comfortable entering an office without having to go through the home. (Figure 3.32) Besides the outside entry, designs for true home office spaces should include generous spaces to accommodate the electronic trappings of a commercial office: computer terminals, modems, printers, telecommunication equipment, copiers, and other equipment.

The diverse spaces of the privacy component provide a typical household with places of retreat. At the other extreme is the ceremonial component, a very public series of formal spaces for the entertainment—and sometimes containment—of guests and visitors.

4

The Ceremonial Component: Entry, Living, and Dining

In every society there is a need for rituals that depart from day-to-day activities. These ceremonies remind us that we are not only individuals but part of a larger whole of families and communities. In our public places we see ceremonies occur in stadiums, theaters, and churches. Inside our homes, they occur in the *entry, living,* and *dining rooms.* (Figure 4.1)

The ceremonial component of a home is used for special occasions, such as formal entertaining, special get-togethers, and other social events. On a percentage basis, these rooms are not heavily used, but when they are, it is for a major event. These rooms are much like a stadium, such as the Rose Bowl; although the big game occurs only once each year, it is a major event that millions of people watch.

In the ceremonial component, the *living* and *dining rooms* demand primarily functional configurations, while the *entry* must include drama as a baseline requirement. Buyer surveys confirm that buyers strongly prefer the community component to face the rear of the lot; the same surveys indicate that buyers prefer that the living and dining rooms face the *front,* which endorses the ceremonial component's role and location as part of the public domain.

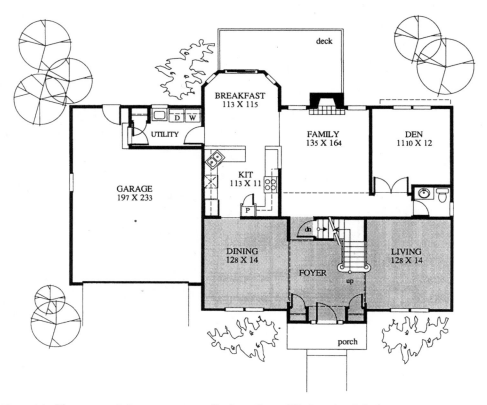

Figure 4.1 The *ceremonial component* usually faces the public domain of the lot.

Entry Area

A design requirement for the entry area is that it convey a feeling of invitation, and often drama. As the place for first impressions, within seconds the entry will afford visitors a positive or negative sense of an environment. The entry is also the location of *last* impressions, and although it is meant to be no more than a place for brief stops before entering or leaving the home, it is in fact more than that. Incoming guests may use the area only briefly, but departing guests often linger here, particularly after a successful and pleasant evening, repeating their thanks and farewells. Thus, the entry also acts as a type of "holding area" before departures.

Design of the entry area begins outside the house with the *front door*. Careful design of the front door includes determining which way the door will swing, the goal being to assure the visitor an optimal initial view. Increasingly, sidelights are standard for at least one side of the door to allow natural light into the entry and as a way for household occupants to preview the visitors outside. (Figure 4.2)

Figure 4.2 The entry is commonly the focal point of the front elevation.

Rather than being the first in a series of rooms, the *entry* often is used as the common thread between the main rooms of the ceremonial component— the *living* and *dining rooms.* In many cases, it will be located in the middle of the ceremonial component with guests directed immediately to the proper station at the left or right (living or dining). (Figure 4.3)

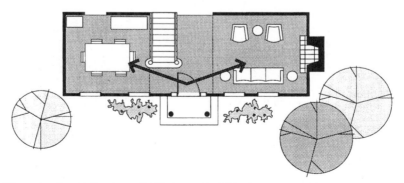

Figure 4.3 The entry foyer often is centrally located within the ceremonial component for optimal initial views of the interior as well as for circulation.

In the entry itself, all *sight lines* should be thoroughly scrutinized. The goal is to create a gracious initial view of the house which conveys spaciousness. Commonly, this is achieved by designing for views open to the largest possible combination of spaces, both *horizontal and vertical*. Views of the operational centers of the home (kitchens, utility rooms, and so on) often mean views of disorder. Like powder rooms, garages, or closets, these elements should not be directly visible from the entry. (Figure 4.4)

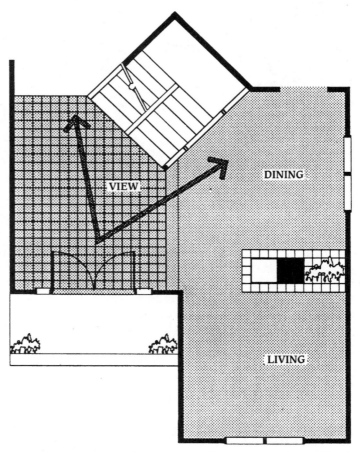

Figure 4.4 The immediate view from the entry should be scrutinized carefully. Avoid views of utilitarian spaces; instead, display the home's spaciousness.

In two-story homes, locating the *stairs* in the entry often allows for the introduction of higher ceilings and a sense of drama. Often the *stair hall* may be the only large-volume space in the entire home. A two-story entry hall is ideal for second-level overlooks—and specialty windows that add natural light and views to this space. (Figure 4.5)

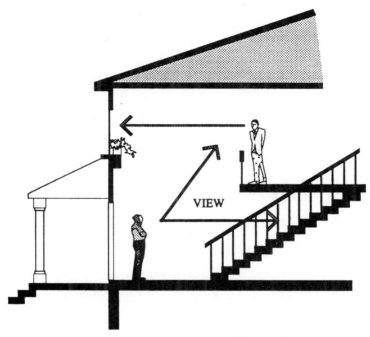

Figure 4.5 Often the entry stair hall is a two-story space, allowing for extensive vertical and horizontal views.

In addition to satisfying the aesthetic considerations of the entry hall, component design must accommodate several functional requirements. An accessible *coat closet* should be near the entry door, particularly in northern climates. This rule is often violated, particularly in southern climates. Too often, coat closets are an afterthought for designers and are either omitted or squeezed into a small, inconvenient place at the last minute. Coat closets should have at least 3 linear feet of rod and shelf, with a 4-foot dimension being preferable. The closet door should be at least 2-feet wide, with generous space in front for easy maneuvering. (Figure 4.6)

The entry hall is also an ideal location for the *powder room*. Also called a *half bath,* the powder room is a basic program requirement for even very small two-level houses when all other bathrooms are on the second level. Increasingly, a separate powder room is standard for ranch-style homes as well, so that visitors do not need to visit a primary bathroom and view the occupant's private domain.

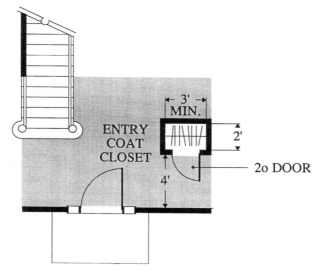

Figure 4.6 It is important to locate a reasonably-sized coat closet in the entry foyer near the front door.

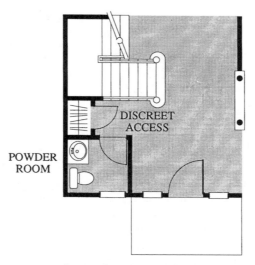

Figure 4.7 Discreet access to the powder room can be achieved easily from the entry foyer. Be sure the initial view from the front door does not include the inside of the powder room, however.

The foremost objective in locating the powder room is to allow for discreet access. Nobody wants to announce, "Well, I am going to the bathroom now," before using this facility. Guests want to be able to slip away from a conversation without being noticed. Locating the powder room in a circulation space such as the entry hall will provide for this kind of accessibility. If square footage allows, plans can include an abbreviated hallway or jog in the plan so that the bathroom is recessed from the foyer to promote further privacy. (Figure 4.7)

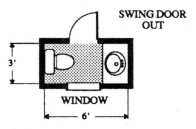

RECTANGULAR POWDER ROOM

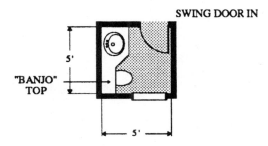

SQUARE POWDER ROOM

Figure 4.8 Efficient powder room shapes can be square or rectangular. Try to include a window in the powder room as well.

If possible, the powder room should include *a window.* As with any bathroom, natural ventilation and light is appealing and beneficial; in the small dimensions of a powder room, this is particularly true. But because the powder room is used minimally, a window is not vitally important to the success of its room's design. Traditionally, the powder room has been extremely small, most often 3 feet by 5 feet or 4 feet by 4 feet. In most markets, a 3-foot-by-6-foot or 5-foot-by-5-foot space is better, as it can accommodate a vanity and toilet side by side. Popular current options for the powder room include elegant "pedestal" vanities or "banjo" vanity tops that partially cover the toilet. Note however, that in small, affordable homes, the powder room size can and should be *minimal,* so as not to lose space from adjacent rooms. (Figure 4.8)

As mentioned earlier, the powder room may be paired with a guest suite. When this is the case, the design may include either a *shower/tub* combination or a *shower* and a *window*. Here, providing *compartmentalization* becomes more important. Many times powder room visitors only wash their hands; therefore, a separate vanity is nice. (Figure 4.9)

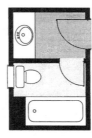

Figure 4.9 A powder room can be compartmentalized between the vanity and the toilet/shower, particularly when it is occasionally used as a full bath for guests.

The design of the powder room should also give careful attention to sound mitigation. Once inside the powder room, guests do not want to feel as if their every move can be heard through paper-thin walls. As with all bathrooms, buffer spaces such as stairs and closets should surround the powder room to help muffle noise.

Formal Living Room

Drawing room, parlor, minister's room—these are some of the various ancestors of today's *formal living room,* a space reserved for the most formal of guests. This is the place for serving afternoon tea, inspecting young suitors, or hosting the card club. (Figure 4.10)

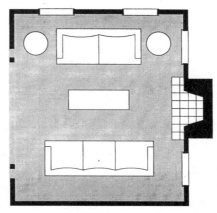

Figure 4.10 A formal living room generally stresses symmetry and balance in the placement of windows, wall openings, and other elements.

With our contemporary society's predominantly informal lifestyle, there is some debate over how valid the formal living room really is today. Certainly, there are very few households that confine their entertainment to the living room. Invariably, guests will avoid spending too much time there if it is possible to drift to where the action is—the kitchen. Thus, one must ask why the living room has been retained over the years. The answer lies partly in tradition, which, despite contemporary lifestyle changes, is still very much a part of consumer values. For most households, formal occasions have become more informal and more infrequent, but even the most casual homeowners enjoy having certain spaces that can rise to the cause of special occasions.

Recognizing the diminishing use of the living room, many contemporary designers are reconfiguring it into a larger freestyle space that may also include the balance of the ceremonial component. As with other traditional movements, this may be more prevalent in the southern climates, where new communities devoted to casual, resort lifestyles favor a plan that combines the living, dining, and entry areas into one *grand room, great room,* or *keeping room.* In plans of relatively small square footage, this trend makes much more sense than the compartmentalization of rooms found in the traditional markets of northern climates. Yet, even with this type of combined space, today's designs are incorporating more formal elements than those of 10 to 15 years ago. (Figures 4.11 and 4.12)

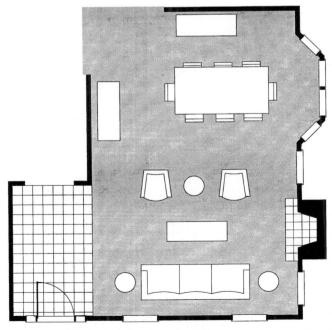

Figure 4.11 A *grand room* includes both the living and dining room in a combined space.

The formal design of the living room also accommodates its role as the *household museum* or *gallery*. Here, the finest furniture, artwork, and heirlooms can be shown in their full splendor. They enhance the living room, and the room complements them. In family households, this formality also discourages high-volume traffic, which protects these family treasures.

When the *museum* role is acknowledged for the living room, several design objectives become apparent, whether the living room is a separate room or just an area in part of the great room. Like an art gallery, the room should include *ample wall space* for display purposes. Door and window placements that create interior symmetry and balanced dimensions within the room promote a formal sense for this space. The size of the living room depends largely on market preferences and price limitations. In very small houses, the living room can be adequately accommodated in a 12- by 12-foot space, but a

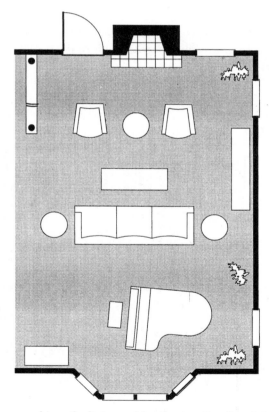

Figure 4.12 A *great room* combines the living and family room functions into a single, comfortable space.

14- by 14-foot space is more acceptable. Although some designs introduce *volume ceilings* into the living room, buyers will prefer emphasis on materials and treatments, such as *moldings* and upgraded *wall veneers*. (Figure 4.13)

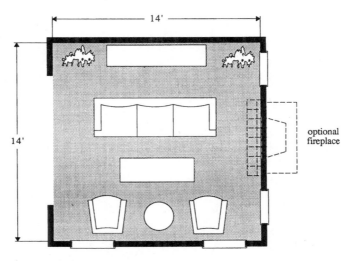

Figure 4.13 The traditional living room often favors symmetry and ample wall space for display purposes.

Fireplaces for the living room are still very popular but are increasingly offered as an option or are included as a secondary fireplace after the one in the family room. The location of the *fireplace, windows,* and *openings* must be carefully considered, as the living room's primary requirement is to accommodate furniture for comfortable seating that promotes conversation. The placement of windows in the living room should recognize that the people using this room will often be seated; here, lower, narrower windows afford views as well as light to seating areas. Skylights and clerestory (higher) windows also add illumination and interest and are especially helpful in smaller living room plans.

Seating areas in the living room should be large enough to contain a sofa and side chairs, with a fireplace and/or specialty windows as the focal point of the furniture arrangement. Balancing the room to include a sufficient amount of wall area, furnishing space, and windows is vitally important to the effective design of the living room. An overabundance of windows here will undoubtedly force the owners to partially cover a window with a sofa or chair. The most sensible solution designates one wall as a *view wall,* and one or two walls as *furniture walls.* A good-view exposure should be assigned to the view wall with the furniture wall left blank. The view wall may also include the *fireplace,* which gives the room a focus for either day or evening use. (Figure 4.14)

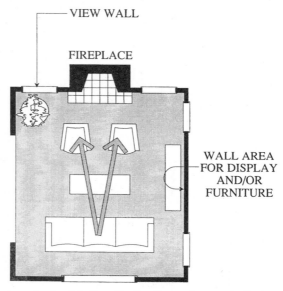

Figure 4.14 Living room layouts should allow for furniture placements that promote views and conversation.

Dining Room

For many of today's households, the *dining room* plays only a vestigial role in daily life. Fewer households gather regularly for evening meals, and most singles and empty-nesters will bemoan how little time they spend preparing genuine evening meals. For most households, formal dining is also much less important. In response to this trend of increasingly casual lifestyles, some designers and builders have reduced the dining room to a modest area within a grand room, even in large estate homes.

In recent years buyers have again begun to demand a "real" dining room, and today's larger new homes include either a dining room that is separate from the living room or a more formal design treatment for the dining area of a great room floor plan. As with the living room, when the separate dining room is utilized, it is reserved for special occasions. In fact, the infrequency of its use contributes to the significance of the meals that are shared there. Its importance is heightened by the fact that it is the backdrop for the oldest and most enduring of social rituals—*offering hospitality through the medium of food*. Because of this context, the dining room is the epitome of the ceremonial component, and minimal attention to its design will not suffice.

As with the living room, the dining room should emphasize grace and dignity; this is attained through *window placements, quality finishes,* and *quality materials*. Because of the room's limited use, and because much of that use occurs during evening hours, provision for prime views to the outdoors is nice, but not mandatory. And because most use is at night, the dining room is the only room in the house equipped with a fancy light fixture as standard equipment. If handsome views are available within the overall context of the floor plan, window placement should be low enough so that the views can be enjoyed from a seated position.

The dimensions for the dining room should be no less than 12 by 12 feet, and a 14- by 14-foot space is far more comfortable. A rectangular configuration, say 12 by 14 feet, is also very functional as most dining room tables are rectangular. Enriching the design of what is essentially a straightforward space is best achieved through specialty window treatments; these may include a bay window or window seat, clerestory windows, or arched windows. Since the dining room is often part of the front elevation, these distinctive touches create additional interest and appeal in the exterior facade. (Figure 4.15)

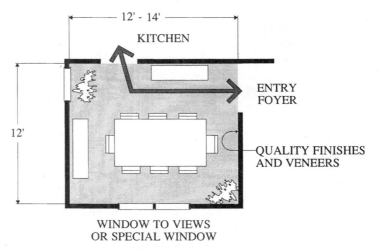

Figure 4.15 The formal dining room should be sized for clearances around the table but have circulation paths that avoid going around the table.

As with the living room, the dining area needs *adequate wall space* for furniture placement. A location for a *hutch* or *china closet* should be designed, as well as for a lower *serving table.* In smaller dining rooms, built-ins can assume these roles with *shelves, buffet countertops,* and *closed cupboards* incorporated into one wall. Whether for small or large gatherings, the dining room should also provide plenty of space for trays and other serving pieces and enough room to maneuver chairs successfully in and out from the table. (Figure 4.16)

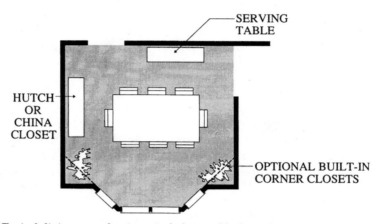

Figure 4.16 Typical dining room furniture includes a table for eight, a server, and a china closet or hutch.

Access to the kitchen is extremely important to the function of the dining room. Some separation from the utilitarian base for an elegant meal is certainly desirable, and views from the dining room should not include a direct sight-line into the kitchen. But too great a distance is impractical and exasperating. In most households, the host and hostess are also the cooks and servers. Even if they have assistants to bring and remove food and dinnerware, the host and hostess will probably have to supervise some of this activity. In either case, appreciable walking distance to and from the kitchen is undesirable.

Some designers believe that the distance from the kitchen to the formal dining room can be lengthy, because the dining room is so seldom used; they argue for a remote location that captures a dramatic view or other amenity. Many home buyers do not agree with this opinion and will likely object if the distance exceeds 12 to 14 feet from the kitchen work triangle.

The ceremonial component represents the center stage of houses. To perform properly, this theater must be supported by a backstage area that functions with maximum efficiency—the functional component.

5

The Functional Component: Laundry, Storage, Garage, Basement, and Attic

Behind every successful restaurant is an efficient kitchen; off the showroom floor, even the glossiest automobile dealerships have a service department; hotels refer to service areas as "the back of the house." And in our homes, we have service and storage areas—also known as the *functional component*. (Figure 5.1)

Typically, the functional component includes a *one, two, or three-car garage,* a *laundry area,* and *storage spaces* which may include parts of a *basement, attic,* or *unfurnished rooms.* These spaces generally aren't visually appealing, but they are very important to home buyers, and must be designed with the same care as the rest of the home. As with other components of the home, each element of the functional component has special design requirements.

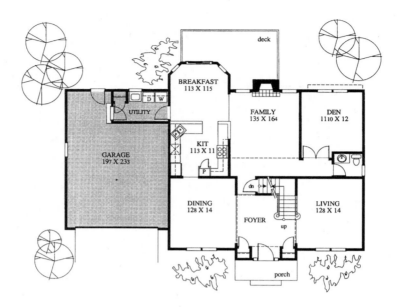

Figure 5.1 The functional component includes utility rooms, garages, basements, attics, and unfinished spaces.

Laundry

Almost every home includes provisions for washing clothes. Historically, the laundry room was located in the basement (if there was a basement), in the garage, or in a remote utility closet. In contemporary homes, the emphasis on convenience has moved the laundry closer to the main living quarters.

In ranch-style homes generally we find the laundry room near the master or secondary bedroom block or in a *mudroom* space between the kitchen and the garage. In two-story homes with all the bedrooms on the second level, the laundry is off the second floor hall or in the traditional first-floor mudroom. In two-story homes with the master bedroom downstairs, the laundry is also downstairs, often near the master suite. (Figure 5.2)

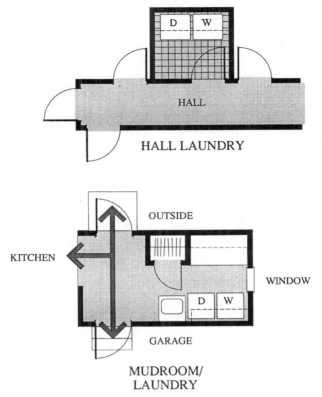

Figure 5.2 The second-floor-hall laundry is sometimes preferred for homes with all the bedrooms upstairs. The traditional location in most markets, however, is the mudroom, located off the kitchen and garage with direct access to the outside.

According to many home buyer surveys, the *first floor mudroom* is still the favored location for the laundry. For maximum convenience, empty-nesters and mature households prefer their laundry near the bedrooms. But in all cases these are preferences, not imperatives. The pros and cons of each of these various laundry locations will be affected by lifestyle preferences and other trade-offs as the home's overall layout evolves.

If the house layout permits, an outside wall location within the laundry will allow for a *window,* which pleasantly enhances a room used for an inescapable chore. In many mid-sized homes, however, the laundry should be relegated to an interior location so that other, more habitable rooms have access to windows. One popular use of the mudroom is for circulation to the garage and/or the outside the house, particularly in areas where harsh weather is a factor. An extremely efficient layout will align the washer/dryer along one wall and provide counter space on the other, with circulation in between. (Figure 5.3)

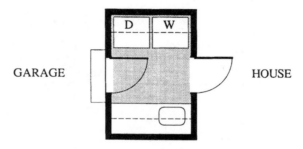

GARAGE   HOUSE

Figure 5.3 Space within a mudroom often is used effectively for circulation, particularly in smaller homes.

As discussed earlier, the laundry is one of the major noise generators in a home and should be buffered from adjacent rooms. Care should be taken to avoid making the plumbing wall of the laundry a party wall to adjacent rooms. If possible, a closet or garage wall should share the laundry's plumbing wall. (Figure 5.4)

When other locations are used for the laundry, designs should focus on similar objectives: noise isolation and windows. When the laundry is near bedrooms, it is sometimes reduced to a small closet to economize on space. This may be necessary in some smaller houses but is not an optimal arrangement for houses over 2000 square feet. When laundry closets *are* used, it is nice to have a linen closet nearby. (Figure 5.5)

Figure 5.4 Locating the mudroom next to the garage will help keep the noise of the washer and dryer away from the rest of the house.

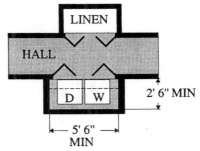

Figure 5.5 In smaller homes, a laundry closet often is located in a hallway where it is convenient to bedrooms.

Other small-home designs locate the laundry in a closet off the kitchen/breakfast area or inside the second bath. (Figure 5.6) Both of these solutions are far from ideal and should be avoided in larger houses, but may be workable in smaller, affordable homes. Further, people with certain household profiles prefer to have laundry areas near other rooms where they may be able to work on food preparation or other projects while doing the laundry. Noise isolation, however, is more often the priority.

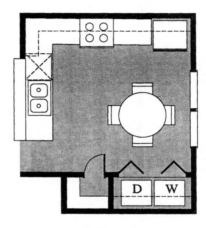

**LAUNDRY IN
KITCHEN**

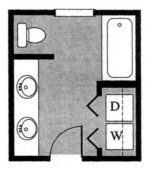

**LAUNDRY
IN BATH**

Figure 5.6 Locating laundry areas within the kitchen or bathrooms is common for affordable homes and for small-home market, but generally is not ideal for larger houses.

In some traditional markets, builders have tended to cling to the basement or garage as a laundry location; although designers may question this, accommodating buyer preference is more sensible than forcing an unwanted change.

When a separate laundry room is included in a house, it is often too small to be truly effective—perhaps a 6- by 6-foot room with just enough space for the washer and dryer, plus circulation. (Figure 5.7) An increase in this area, however, yields a tremendous return, both in terms of function and appeal. Enlarging this space to allow for an *island work table* and room to maneuver will make doing the laundry much easier. If the mudroom concept is selected, design should include space for both a washer and a dryer, *counter space* for folding clothes, *overhead cabinets, a laundry tub,* and possibly *a small closet.* These elements require a space approximately 7 by 12 feet. In homes designed for families, larger laundry space is especially important as children continually generate mountains of wash. (Figure 5.8)

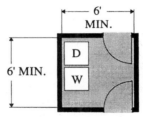

Figure 5.7 A minimal laundry room needs a space about six feet square.

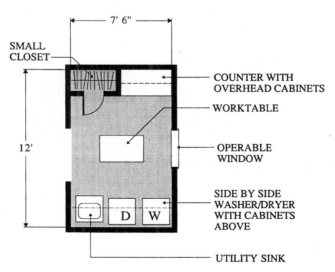

Figure 5.8 A more generous laundry will include a utility sink, small closet, cabinets and counter space, and a worktable. Try to include a window as well.

Storage

Before beginning the specific discussion of storage elements in the functional component, we should state the general role that *more is better* and it's almost impossible to have too much! The accoutrements of all but the most spartan lifestyle are plentiful, and more people will admit to being pack rats than to keeping their possessions to a minimum. In addition, few people find the time to regularly weed out accumulated possessions. *Consumer surveys have indicated that storage space is one of the primary concerns of buyers evaluating potential new homes for purchase.* For these reasons, new home designs should incorporate as much storage as possible, either built-ins or in the form of spaces that provide options for adding cabinets, shelves, closets, cubbyholes, pegboard, hooks, and other storage devices.

Garage

You may have often heard the saying that homeowners pay more to house their automobile than their children. It's true: On a square-footage basis, the garage generally is the largest single space in a home. More important, it must occupy valuable ground-level space.

Like other components in contemporary homes, the garage has recently expanded its role. Although one-car garages were once common even for homes in the 2000-square-foot range, two-car garages are now almost always standard for detached homes above 1400 square feet; and in some markets, three-car garages are common for houses over 2500 square feet. Over 70 percent of all new homes have garage space for two or more cars. Interestingly, in most cases at least one bay of the two or three-car garage is devoted to storage.

The space provided in most plans for the two-car garage is 20 by 20 feet, which is tight for two domestic cars and the maneuvering they require. If two cars are to be stored, this leaves little room for the additional necessities kept in the garage—the lawn mower, garden equipment, auto repair paraphernalia, and just plain junk. By increasing one of the garage dimensions to 23 or 24 feet, a 3- to 4-foot strip can be allocated for storing these items. (Figure 5.9)

A *workshop space* within the garage is often popular, particularly in floor plans without basements. To accommodate this option, the garage dimensions should be increased from the 20-foot minimum to 24 feet, with wall space reserved for pegboards and some windows for natural light. Regardless of whether a workshop will be included in the garage plan, it should have at

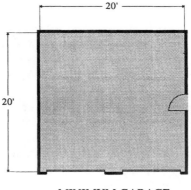

MINIMUM GARAGE

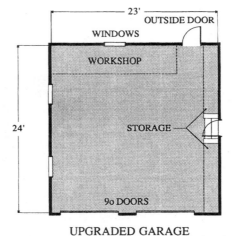

UPGRADED GARAGE

Figure 5.9 Increasing garage dimensions beyond the 20- by 20-foot minimum (for a two-car garage) will allow room for the additional necessities that need to be stored there. Other amenities for garages include windows, 9-foot overhead doors, and outdoor access via a swing door.

least one window and a swing door for outdoor access, separate from the overhead garage door.

Although an 8-foot-wide single garage door and a 16-foot-wide double garage door are standard, increasing these widths to 9 and 18 feet, respectively, is desirable for larger move-up homes. *Automatic garage door openers* are also becoming standard, as are *pull-down stairs* for rafter storage above, particularly in houses without basements.

Basement

Traditionally, basements have been standard in single-family homes in the northern states. Because of structural customs, this is unlikely to change, although affordability issues are promoting some slab-on-grade designs. Also by tradition, the basement has been designed with about as much aesthetic appeal and living potential as a coal chute.

Where basements are standard, designers and builders should devote some marketing consideration to the potential this area has for uses other than mechanical equipment and storage. Designs should anticipate the location of a *future recreation room* that could consume up to 50 percent of the total area, but still leave ample room for *equipment* and *storage*. A "rec room" would expand the capacity of the community component and give parents the option of relegating noisy packs of children and teens to a more remote area of the home. Higher ceilings, windows, and wall insulation are becoming prevalent in the basements of larger move-up homes to permit even more successful conversion of this space to casual living uses. (Figure 5.10)

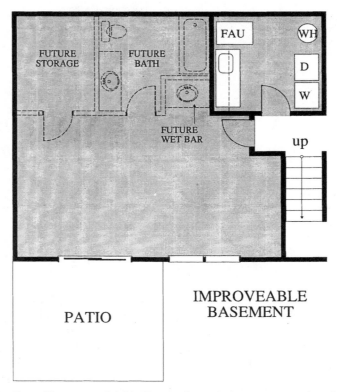

Figure 5.10 A "walk-out" basement should allow for future improvements such as bathrooms, wet bars, and walled-off storage areas.

Providing 9-foot ceilings in basements facilitates this type of remodeling and is becoming standard in the design programs for new homes of over 3000 square feet. Raising the home's first floor to around 3 feet above grade is also worth considering; this allows more light into the basement and adds significant appeal to areas converted to living space. (Figure 5.11)

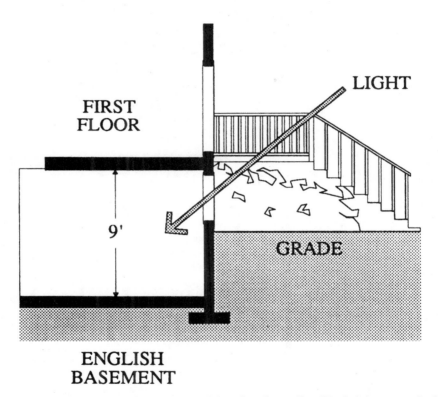

FIRST FLOOR

LIGHT

GRADE

9'

ENGLISH BASEMENT

Figure 5.11 Higher basement ceilings and raised first floor lines allow "English basements" which bring natural light into the lower level to enhance their appeal.

For sloped sites, *walk-out basements* can be incorporated and marketed for appropriate uses. These plans include windows and doors on the rear "downhill" side of the basement for light, views and outdoor access. Further, a potential bath area or wet bar should be included in the rough-plumbing layout for potential future improvement.

Attic Storage

In sunbelt homes or other markets where basements are not traditionally provided, *attics* become very important as storage locations. Access to attic storage is commonly provided by way of *pull-down stairs* from a hall location or from a bedroom in smaller homes. (Try to keep the location of a pull-down staircase in a low-visibility location, away from formal areas.) In larger homes, attic access is provided by a *full stairway.* (Figure 5.12) Higher exterior roof pitches and dormer windows reflect the impact of this trend on elevations. Many designers are also including plywood floors in the attic, with some even providing insulation that will allow for future upgrading of this space for use as a recreation room, study, or auxiliary bedroom.

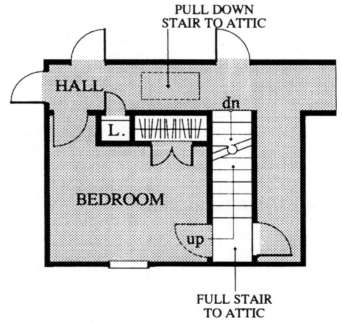

Figure 5.12 In markets without basements, a full staircase to the attic is highly desirable. Other times, a pull-down staircase will suffice for access to this space.

The functional component is possibly the most neglected series of spaces in terms of design. Because of its mundane character, it is often overlooked, undersized, or forgotten. But in a well-designed home, it will contribute to the enjoyment of living as much as the other, more visible components.

6

The Outdoor Component: Yards, Curb Appeal, and Neighborhood Context

The housing design process must include careful attention to the homes' surrounding environment, beginning with the individual lot and extending through the street and neighborhood. The ultimate goal is to produce an external fabric that promotes a sense of community as well as privacy. Immediate outdoor environs are a natural and usable extension of internal living space, often expanding from the floor plan's structural envelope to become the *outdoor component*. (Figure 6.1)

In order to provide truly usable outdoor space, the public/private duality of the lot, otherwise known as the *front yard* and *back yard,* must be defined. Many high-density planning concepts have altered the definition of the traditional front/rear orientations, particularly with the introduction of *zero-lot-line houses* which use a single side yard as a privacy area. (Figure 6.2) Even with these lot variations, the design and planning of the outdoor component must balance public and private relationships.

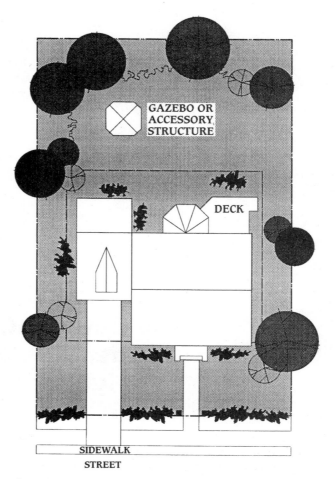

Figure 6.1 The *outdoor component* encompasses the area surrounding the house, including the lot and extending through the street and neighborhood.

As previously mentioned, home buyer surveys have indicated that people prefer that the kitchen and family rooms face the rear of the lot. Landscaping for this part of the outdoor component must reinforce privacy and stress livable, but secluded, outdoor spaces. Both physical and visual access to the private yard should be linked to the community component and should not be easily seen from adjacent homes. Although detailed treatment of the rear elevation is rare in most markets, establishing a design character for this part of the house should not be ignored. The frequency of its use justifies detailing it as well as the front.

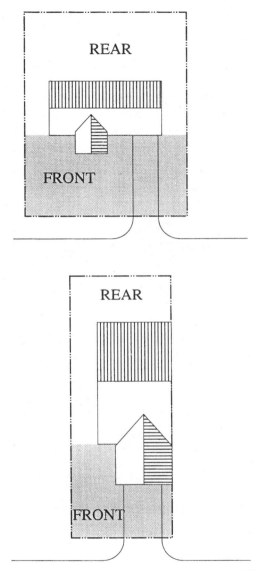

Figure 6.2 The traditional front/rear orientation of yards has been modified with zero-lot-line houses and other narrow-lot concepts.

Deck/Patio

The rear deck or patio area is very popular with homeowners, and when properly designed, it becomes an outdoor "room" with intrinsic appeal for outdoor relaxation, dining, and entertaining. The *rear deck* has many regional variations, from the Florida-style *lanai* to the *screened porch* of the middle states and the *sunroom* of the northern states. Each has the objective of providing an enjoyable outdoor or semi-outdoor area with easy access to the interior of the house. (Figures 6.3 and 6.4)

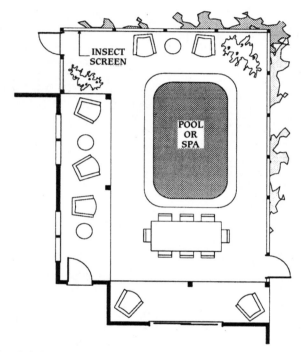

Figure 6.3 In sunbelt locations, the outdoor lanai incorporates an entire swimming pool within a large screened enclosure.

Figure 6.4 A screened-in porch may have removable glass panels which are used to convert the space into a sunroom during colder months.

Decks or patios should be dimensioned generously; optimal sizes are often 12 to 14 feet deep and 16 to 24 feet wide. To facilitate their use as outdoor living areas, decks should be designed in much the same fashion as other interior rooms by accommodating potential furniture layouts for dining, conversation, and circulation. (Figure 6.5) Decks should also be placed to capture the site's prime vistas but should not block views from major interior rooms. *Multiple-level decks* are indicative of the increased attention and value of the outdoor component. With these designs, the dining area may be at a different level from the rest of the deck, with planters and/or decorative railings employed to define the different uses. (Figure 6.6)

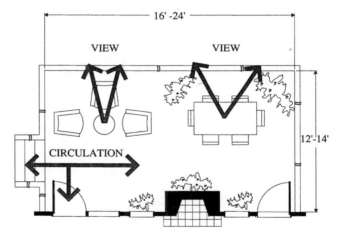

Figure 6.5 Much like an interior room, outdoor deck and patio design should accommodate furniture and circulation paths.

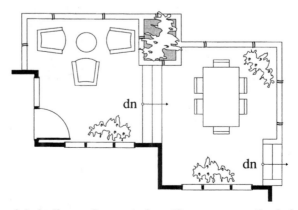

Figure 6.6 A multilevel deck allows refinement of specific-use areas on the deck.

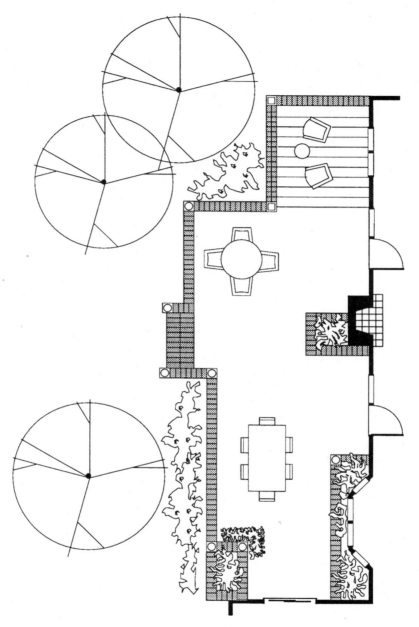

Figure 6.7 Larger homes often have extensive, grade-level patios defined by planters, trellis structures, and low garden walls.

Although they are traditionally constructed of concrete, ground-level patios in larger homes often incorporate upgraded materials, such as brick, granite, and flagstone. Low brick walls can further define and dignify the outdoor patio, while wood trellises and planters provide decorative enrichment. (Figure 6.7)

In warmer climates, the optimal arrangement of the outdoor components includes space for a *pool* or *spa*. Regional market variations will determine the shape and location of this feature, which embodies dual roles as a landscape *and* a recreational element. For larger homes, a water feature will often be a *reflecting pool,* which provides elegance and a serene focal point for outdoor spaces. Lap pools that provide year-round opportunities for exercise are also popular, particularly in mature markets. If a *spa* is to be part of the outdoor component, it should be easily accessible to one of the bathrooms; in many cases this bath includes a door with direct access to the outside. Direct access from the master bath is also desirable. (Figure 6.8)

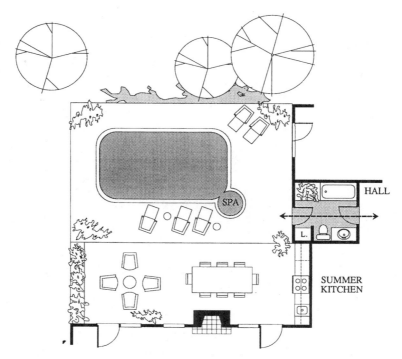

Figure 6.8 Direct access to an interior bathroom from the pool area is desirable in sunbelt markets that include pools.

Like the interior of the home, outdoor dining areas should consider travel distances to and from the kitchen. *Pass-throughs* or outdoor *serving areas* should be incorporated into the deck layout. More important, however, is the optimal location for an *outdoor grill.* Smoke and ashes wafting through the dining area may not be completely avoidable with the traditional open-air deck, but consideration of the prevailing breezes can minimize this problem. A *built-in grill* along one exterior wall with an exhaust stack virtually eliminates this problem, and is an increasingly popular feature, particularly in sunbelt lanais. In more upscale homes, the outdoor grill is part of a separate *summer kitchen,* which includes a sink and refrigerator as well for full-service outdoor dining. (Figure 6.8)

Landscaping

Beyond the hard surfaces of the yard—deck, patio, and pool—we have the balance of the lot available for landscaping material. In most markets, lifestyle preferences dictate *low-maintenance landscaping.* In fact, there is a growing trend for outdoor yard areas to be maintained by a homeowners' association, even in detached-home communities. By contrast, the *home and garden movement,* which calls for elaborately landscaped outdoor areas with fences, walkways, and planting areas that integrate exterior design with the plan of the house, is still alive and well in regions that favor traditional designs.

Traditionally, the rear yard was maintained as a grass lawn with intermittent shrubs for privacy or accents. Recent lifestyle preferences favor preserving a more natural-looking site, particularly in wooded or desert areas. Here, sodded grass may be installed as an ornamental feature that will be more important to look at than to use. In arid desert climates, landscaping that minimizes water use is very much in favor.

Other landscape goals focus on the need to partially or completely enclose the private yard areas with shrubs and trees that will screen the outdoor areas from neighboring homes. (Figure 6.9)

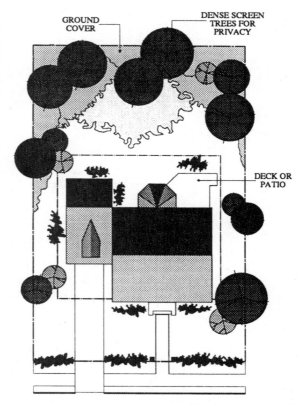

Figure 6.9 For wooded lots, minimal landscaping may be all that is needed. In other cases, screen landscaping should be added to enhance privacy in yard areas.

Entry Yard

On the street side of a home, the critical design and planning issues include *curb appeal, entry enhancement,* and *neighborhood context.* As with other design considerations of production housing, designers and home builders are becoming increasingly aware of the importance of these elements of the outdoor component. Real estate agents know that the chances of selling even the most enticing floor plans are diminished by nondescript elevations, landscaping, and awkward streetscapes. Of key interest to prospective buyers is the neighborhood's ambiance and character. Thoughtful design of the elements that define the neighborhood context will contribute to a friendly, personable setting for the houses. (Figure 6.10)

Figure 6.10   The front elevation and yard landscaping should combine to project a friendly image of the house and yard.

Of critical importance is the *garage location.* One major residential design objective should be to minimize the impact of the garage, not only on each of the individual lots but also on the streetscape as a whole. Simultaneously, the design must emphasize the *entry* to the home. Where possible, the garage should be set back from the front elevation, while the entry should project forward.

Attention to the garage as an architectural element, rather than as a necessary evil, is highly advisable. Detailed garage doors with subtle color accents are more appealing than flat, monochromatic treatments, and windows in garage door panels add life to an uninhabited space. Architectural elements of the house itself can also be repeated on or over the garage, to draw the eye up or away from the garage. (Figure 6.11)

Figure 6.11   Keeping the garage to the side and behind the front facade of the house will help minimize its presence. The placement of dormer windows over the garage will also help pull the eye away from garage doors below.

Figure 6.12   The entry is the focal point of many residential elevations. Sidelights, porches, steps, and special windows can all call attention to the entry door.

The primary design focus on the front elevation, however, should be the *entry,* which may include a *covered porch* with *decorative railings, columns,* or *trim.* Often a *specialty window* is located above the entry to further emphasize its significance. The entry should be a major design statement on the front elevation. (Figure 6.12)

Facade Design

Like the entry, the entire street view of the house should be enriched with upgraded veneer material, windows, and pleasing rooflines. Depending on the market and region, exterior forms will be either symmetrical or asymmetrical, a dichotomy generally described earlier as *traditional* or *transitional* design. Even within traditional contexts, designers and builders can sometimes depart from enduring residential forms by introducing new designs that continue to use the materials, colors, and textures favored by buyers who prefer traditional homes. (Figure 6.13)

Figure 6.13 A departure from traditional architectural styles may be softened with designs that maintain traditional colors, materials, and textures that are favored by buyers.

Architectural styles aside, the massing and detailing of the front elevation must be pleasing to the eye. Usually, height connotes value; therefore, two-story facades are found to be preferable with single-level spaces more at the rear of the home. Multiple roof-levels with sloping hip roofs are becoming popular in many regions, along with elaborate specialty windows and porches in the regional style. Consumer surveys indicate that brick is a highly sought-after veneer material, with stone in second place.

Regional historical forms are generally most prevalent in traditionally dominated luxury communities—Spanish Colonial and Mission styles in southern California, saltbox and farmhouse styles in New England, and Georgian or Federal styles in the middle Atlantic and southern states. In those symmetry is often favored, and asymmetrical elevations should be bold in their massing. (Figure 6.14)

Figure 6.14 There is a growing preference among consumers for facades that reflect regionally appropriate architecture.

An important concept to address in facade design is the need to *accentuate the entry*. Recent high-density house/lot designs have moved the front door to the interior of the lot, leaving visitors without a clue as to the entry location. In those cases, landscape design may need to be used to provide entry symbols leading the way to the front door. For most wide-lot homes, however, the facade should clearly identify the front door through generous spaces in front of and around the entry door and include quality veneers and special windows nearby.

The usual design objective for *landscaping* in the entry yard is to frame the house, and landscape materials here should work in concert with elevations to accentuate the entry and downplay the garage. This may translate to low shrubs and flowers along the walkway and taller plants used to screen the driveway and the garage. (Figure 6.15) Care must be taken to ensure that foundation plantings and front-yard landscaping do not grow to proportions that overtake or hide parts of the front elevation.

As for the public side of the house, the entry yard should be compatible with the neighborhood context. Architectural styles or forms that vary too much with prevailing regional designs will not be viewed favorably and should be avoided. At the same time, a sense of individual identity for each new home is desirable; design should promote this goal within the bounds of reasonable precedent. (Figure 6.16)

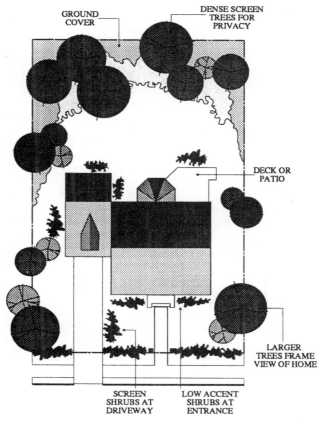

GROUND COVER

DENSE SCREEN TREES FOR PRIVACY

DECK OR PATIO

LARGER TREES FRAME VIEW OF HOME

SCREEN SHRUBS AT DRIVEWAY

LOW ACCENT SHRUBS AT ENTRANCE

Figure 6.15 Landscaping in the entry yard should "frame" the elevation of the house, whereas other landscape materials should enhance privacy within the lot.

The outdoor component is both an extension of the interior living space and a connection to the greater community. Design attention to this portion of a typical house often is lacking; it needs to be given the same level of attention as the inside of the home.

Figure 6.16 Model house designs selected for a community should work together to form a pleasing streetscape.

Synthesis:
Putting It All Together

Following an analysis of each component within a contemporary home is the process of *synthesis:* how to put the components together. Perhaps the most difficult phase in the design process, it requires that the designer balance the complexities of lifestyle goals with the limitations of structure, cost, and other technical concerns. Each component must function properly in two and three-dimensional space, as well as fit within the building envelope established by the lot setbacks.

Any successful synthesis process depends on an understanding of the market group the design is to address. As we will discuss in Chapter 8, different household types and lifestyles express unique preferences for the location and proportion of the various components relative to the overall design.

For all market segments, however, current lifestyle preferences of most households that apply to the synthesis process include:

1. *The domination of informal areas over formal areas.*
2. *The need for style, drama, and places to showcase possessions.*
3. *The interest in expanded kitchens and baths.*
4. *The need for privacy among occupants.*
5. *The need for comfort, practicality, and security that comes with a lifetime investment.*

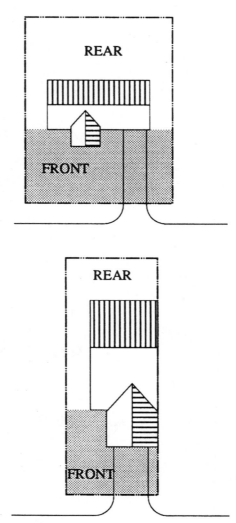

Figure 7.1 Traditional front/rear yard definitions have been altered by small-lot planning concepts. These have dramatically impacted the internal programming of the home.

Public versus Private Orientation

Distinguishing between the *public* and *private* areas of the residential lot is a critical initial consideration of the synthesis process. For a standard rectangular parcel, the answers are obvious: The street side of the lot is public, while the rear portion of the lot is private. Recent trends in designs for small lots and houses, however, have generated other alternatives to this scenario. (Figure 7.1)

Zero-lot-line houses and other small-lot house configurations, such as the *angled Z-lot house,* the *wide-and-shallow-lot house,* the *zipper-lot house,* or the *not-lot house,* have altered traditional public and private orientations. For example, some zero-lot designs may offer more privacy at the *side* of the lot (which faces an adjacent blank wall) instead of the rear yard, which may be compressed and face the open windows of a nearby home. (Figure 7.2) Therefore, a thorough understanding of the house/lot concept is essential prior to the synthesis process of component design.

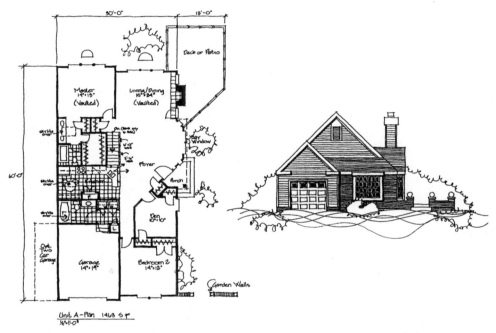

Figure 7.2 Zero-lot-line homes alter the location of the entry by moving it toward the interior of the lot and the back of the house. Therefore, an entry path is needed to direct visitors to the front door.

Establishing Internal Priorities

After public and private lot areas have been clearly identified, the process of assigning interior component locations within the floor plan begins. Which component should get the highest priority for prime views or access to the outdoors? If compromises must occur to fit the program on a small lot, which components should be affected? Further, which components may need to be reduced in size or possibly eliminated in some cases?

Private Orientations

I previously mentioned surveys of buyer preferences for rooms that should receive private orientations. In general, *the community component should always receive a high priority for a privacy orientation.* For households with children, this location generally affords immediate access to a controlled yard area, desirable both for everyday use and for casual entertaining. Indeed, the component where a household spends most of its time deserves top priority for a choice location. (Figure 7.3)

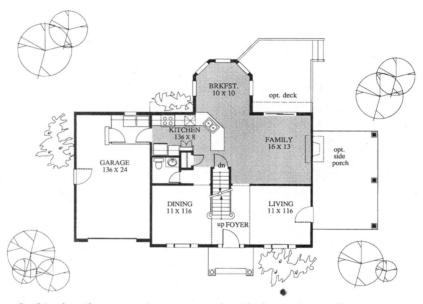

Figure 7.3 In this plan, the community component has ideal rear views and easy access to a private outdoor deck.

For all of the market profiles, however, *the master suite should receive the highest priority for privacy.* Certain benefits should be afforded those who pay the mortgage, and chief among them is that their quarters be well located. For some markets, privacy for the master suite will mean a location well away from the front portion of the home. For others, privacy means a master suite remote from secondary and guest bedrooms. It also generally means a master suite that faces the rear of the lot. (Figure 7.4)

The other privacy component elements—*the secondary bedroom block, guest suite,* and *den/library*—will also benefit from a private orientation but are on a lower priority than the master suite or community component. Indeed, many homes have floor plans where secondary bedrooms and dens face the front or side-yard areas. Also, for houses with den/libraries that are to be used as *home offices,* a public location is preferred, so that visitors may enter the home office immediately upon entering the house, or in some cases from an independent exterior door. (Figure 7.5)

Figure 7.4 If possible, it is always best to have the master bedroom face the private sector of the lot. A degree of separation between the master suite and the secondary bedroom block will enhance the privacy of each.

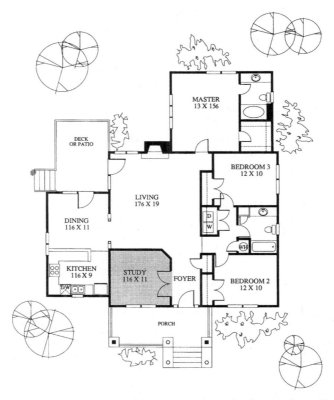

Figure 7.5 For home offices, immediate direct access from the foyer is desirable to minimize the intrusion of business visitors into the home.

Public Orientations

Although the community and privacy components should be in a secluded position, the ceremonial components should face the public sector of the lot. Obviously, the *entry* should face the public domain, allowing visitors to enter the home without immediate access to the private areas. The other formal rooms that make up the ceremonial component—*the living* and *dining rooms*—also generally face the public side of the lot as they typically are connected to the entry. (Figure 7.6)

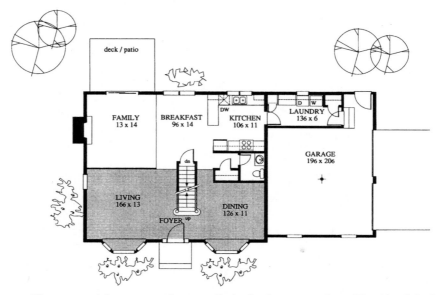

Figure 7.6 The ceremonial component is generally in the front or at the public side of the house with primary rooms connected to the entry hall or foyer.

The ceremonial component location is based on sensible logistics and sound psychology. Even the people we have invited to our home are coming into private territory, and no matter how welcome they are, their arrival is somewhat of an encroachment. When we have not invited the visitor, the intrusion is perceived even more actively. In both cases, the ceremonial component diminishes this feeling by establishing a buffer zone or meeting ground that is less personal than the community and privacy components. Invited visitors often will move on to the community area. Visitors who are not offered more than ritual hospitality will be more comfortable when they are in the neutral territory of the ceremonial component.

Functional Orientations

The rooms whose locations are most flexible are the elements of the functional component: the garage, laundry, work areas, and storage spaces.

The *garage* location will vary dramatically in accordance with the lot-shape, street pattern, and local custom. The traditional location for the garage is at the side of the home, and if lot dimensions permit, a *side-loaded garage* (which buyers prefer) helps to minimize the impact of garage doors on the front elevation. (Figure 7.7) Other schemes that reduce the visual effect of

Figure 7.7 A side-loaded garage is visually more appealing if the lot width allows the driveway to meet the garage at a right angle.

the garage push it to the rear of the house and lot, sometimes as a detached structure or connected to the house via a covered breezeway. (Figures 7.8 and 7.9)

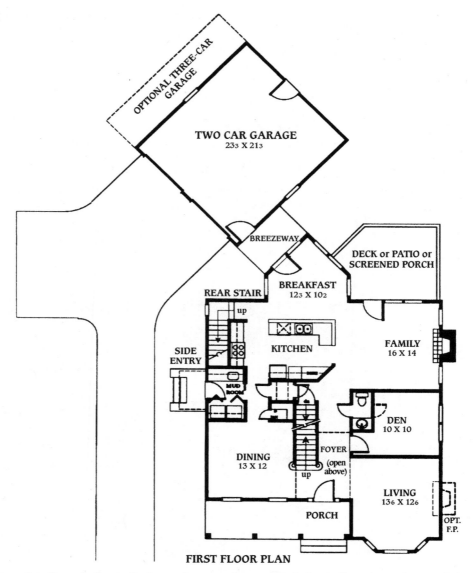

Figure 7.8 One solution to the issue of garage placement is to locate the garage at an angle to a rear corner of the house. This allows the garage to be out of view from the front, but still attached to the house.

Unfortunately, many current small-lot designs require a front-facing garage. Further, narrow-lot schemes generally require that the garage be in front of the home to minimize the amount of the lot area needed for driveways so that the maximum lot area can be devoted to private yards. These

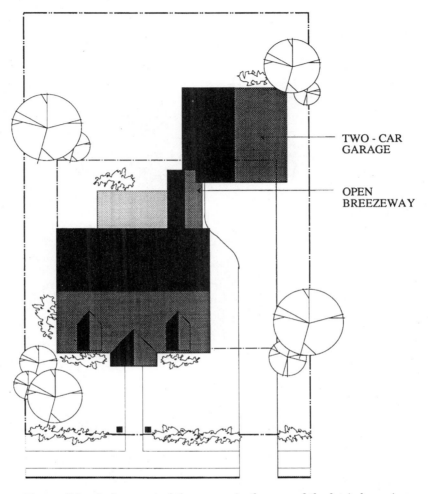

TWO - CAR
GARAGE

OPEN
BREEZEWAY

Figure 7.9 The traditional placement of the garage in the rear of the lot is becoming popular again in some markets. Rear garage placement is ideal to keep cars as far away from the front of the house as possible.

designs require special design considerations, however, to mitigate the visual impact of garages directly on the street and to emphasize the entry location that is removed or hidden from the street. (Figure 7.10)

As mentioned in Chapter 5, the *laundry* or *utility room* location varies according to local market preferences and the house's vertical programming. Both of these factors should be considered carefully and will generally dictate

Figure 7.10 Small lot designs with garages adjacent to the street need special design solutions to mitigate the impact of garage doors. These designs use highly articulated facades and quality paving to maintain a pleasing street scene.

one of the following laundry locations: (1) adjacent to garage, usually as a *mudroom*, or (2) on the second floor of a two-story home, or (3) on the ground floor if the master suite is located on the ground floor also. (Figures 7.11 and 7.12)

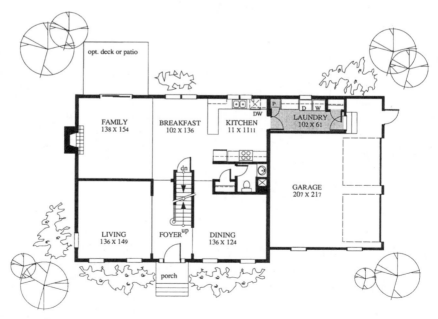

Figure 7.11 The "mudroom" type laundry—convenient to the kitchen and the outside of the house—is preferred by many household profiles.

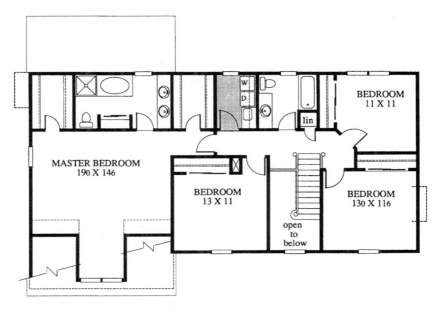

Figure 7.12 A second-floor laundry is preferred when all bedrooms are on the same level.

Relative to orientation, *storage area* locations are the *least* important; relative to our daily living habits, they are among the *most* important. Storage areas should be located where they cause the least interference with the circulation or orientation of the primary components and still are convenient to the components that generate their use. Important locations for short-term storage spaces include the garage for outdoor equipment and within the bedroom blocks for interior items. Long-term storage spaces are found in the attic and/or basement depending on local construction techniques.

Horizontal versus Vertical Priorities

In single-level "ranch" plans, the public and private orientations of components are resolved on one plane. For most floor plans, however, a *second level* is also part of the design program. Often a basement and/or attic can give a house as much as four levels to program.

For homes of two or more levels, determining which components or elements go *up* versus *down* is highly market-specific. For example, for young families, the master suite and secondary bedroom block should be on one level; parents of young children should be able to reach their children easily, since emergencies, night feedings, and illness are recurring factors in attending to the needs of children. (Figure 7.13) Mature households often prefer vertical separation with the master suite down and the secondary bedroom block up. In ranch markets, these two bedroom components are often located on either side of the principal ceremonial and community components affording

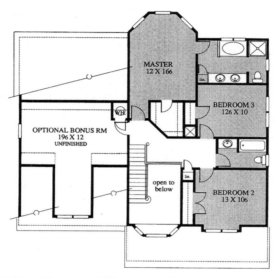

Figure 7.13 Households with young children generally prefer to have all bedrooms on one floor; yet, bedroom doors maintain some degree of separation and privacy.

maximum separation and privacy for both owners and occasional guests. (Figure 7.14)

The use of two or three floors in a housing design can also depend on lot size, views and other site-specific issues. For example, where the *principal view* is to one side, the use of several floors can distribute view access to more components throughout the home. Lots with *sloping topography* often can allow two levels of components to have grade-level outdoor access, rather than just one. These site-specific considerations, however, must be balanced with the market group's internal living preferences.

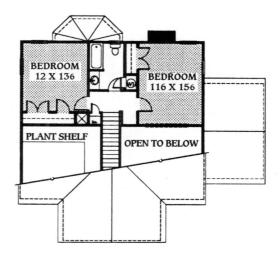

SECOND FLOOR PLAN

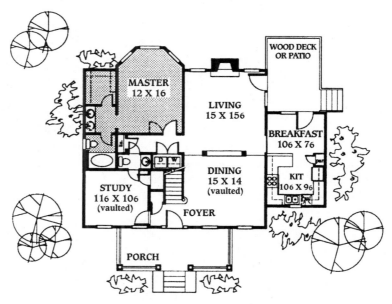

FIRST FLOOR PLAN

Figure 7.14 Mature households often prefer a vertical separation between the master and secondary bedrooms.

Marketing the Third Dimension

When organizing the components of two-story houses, one should consider the general objective of providing some *volume spaces.* In many programs, the square footage required for the first floor is much greater than what is needed for the second floor, so there is ample opportunity to include volume ceilings over several rooms on the first floor.

In organizing either one- or two-story homes, the designer should consider providing at least some volume space, even for very affordable entry-level houses. In larger homes, vaulted ceilings add drama; in smaller homes, volume creates both visual interest and the important illusion that the square footage is greater than it is. This explains the growing popularity of 9-foot ceilings in small condominium and apartment plans, as well as in entry-level starter homes. Many larger, move-up houses now have 10-foot ceilings as a standard feature.

Market group preferences will again dictate the optimal locations for vaulted ceilings, two-story spaces, or overlooks. In almost all markets, the *entry area* or *foyer* rates a high priority for volume. Mature buyers may also favor a vaulted ceiling in the ceremonial component *living* and *dining areas,* whereas younger households generally prefer a vaulted *community component.* In any market, the *master suite* is a popular area in which to include volume space, which adds a bit of grandeur and luxury to this important location.

The amount of volume that is preferred by buyers has been scaled back recently, as more conservative households consider the ongoing energy costs to heat and/or cool more cubic footage. Also, people are not fond of living in spaces that feel too drafty and barnlike. The popularity of *level volume spaces*, where 10- or 12-foot flat ceilings are carried throughout, has increased compared to the sloped vaulted ceilings that reach up to 16 or 18 feet in height. On the other hand, in luxury houses for mature households, designs with *full two-story spaces* in not only the foyer, but portions of the community or ceremonial component as well, have become very popular. (Figure 7.15)

Figure 7.15 Volume spaces are popular in different components within the house depending on market group preferences.

Structural and Technical Considerations

Although lifestyle concerns have recently been given a higher priority in housing designs, construction issues are far from forgotten in the process of organizing components within a home. Obviously, the configuration of rooms that ultimately results in a house must accommodate structural framing modules, plumbing and mechanical stacks, and cost-per-square-foot guidelines. Lifestyle issues may influence, but not control, the necessary technical requirements of structure and mechanical systems. (Figure 7.16)

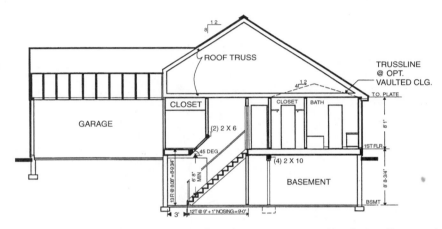

Figure 7.16 Technical considerations are far from forgotten in component design. Structural modules, mechanical stacks, and cost control are very important, particularly in affordable housing.

In affordable housing prototypes, an efficient rectangular shape with a reasonable amount of volume space is currently a popular design solution. Stacking the plumbing walls, limiting the variations in floor joist spans, and creating a feasible envelope and efficient roof system are other important ways to keep costs down in affordable housing.

Synthesis: A Balancing Act

Organizing the components of a typical home into a coherent whole is a difficult process, primarily because the only homes that can give buyers exactly what they envision are custom designed. For most buyers, the purchasing decision will be based on the choices available among production houses. But to produce affordable homes, builders obviously do not have the option of including everything buyers may desire.

These facts generate constraints on virtually every component for living, in terms of size, orientation, and special features. Both designer and builder must approach the process with a sound understanding of market profiles, regional preferences, construction costs, and a method for deciding which program elements are most important to fulfill their market's expectations.

Balancing the objectives of component design with the realities of cost requires much time and thought. A careful approach, however, can pay big dividends to those who are building housing today, and ultimately, to the buyers and occupants of today's new homes.

8

Target Marketing:
Variations on a Theme

The balancing act of synthesis, discussed in Chapter 7, also includes the goal of tailoring the various components to the needs of the *new households,* discussed in Chapter 1. As market research continues to become more sophisticated, broad profiles of the new households with different lifestyle preferences may be accompanied by numerous subsets known as *market niches.* Each of these niches belongs to one of four general household categories.

To discuss fine-tuning component designs to meet the needs of the new households, let us begin by considering the household groups mentioned earlier in Chapter 1:

Group I: Couples with children.

Group II: Couples without children.

Group III: Singles/mingles.

Group IV: Single parents.

Remember that within each of these groups are subgroups, categorized by age and income, as well as regional preferences, and behavior and value differences. So let's discuss how component design can tailor floor plans to meet the needs of these niche markets.

Group I: Couples With Children

Within *Group I* are *young families* looking for starter homes, as well as *mature households* fulfilling the need to move up to a larger home because their family is expanding in size and/or their income is rising.

Young families tend to give a high priority to the design of the *community component*. Although the owners may want formal living and dining rooms as well as family and breakfast areas, the financial limitations of the first-time buyer will usually dictate some sacrifice, particularly in the ceremonial component. For parents of infants and young children, a roomy breakfast nook—one that can even be thought of as a "mini-family room"—will be used more heavily and will add more convenience to daily living than a large, elegant formal dining room. (Figure 8.1)

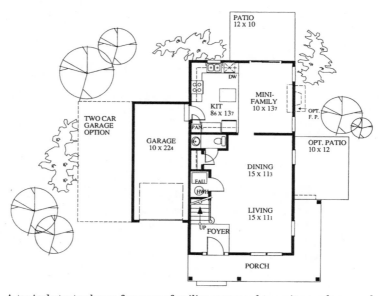

Figure 8.1 A typical starter home for young families may need to omit or reduce much of the ceremonial component because of budget considerations. A popular plan for this group has a combined living/dining space and an expanded breakfast room that can act as a mini-family room. Options to expand the house are also popular.

The family room, or great room, is more vital to the young *Group I* household than the formal ceremonial space of a living room and should be large enough to accommodate the activities of both family members and occasional guests, who probably will include both adults and children. Direct access from this area to the outdoor component is imperative, as are views to this room from the kitchen and breakfast area. Since even a part-time commitment to child tending can be all-consuming and exhausting, those who supervise the children appreciate a vantage point that fulfills safety considerations without requiring total immersion in the hub of activity. (Figures 8.2 and 8.3)

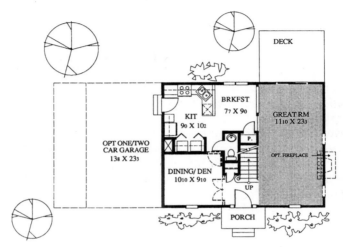

Figure 8.2 A large *great room* is often the most used part of the community component in starter home plans. In this plan, the option of omitting the dining room and using it as a den is suggested.

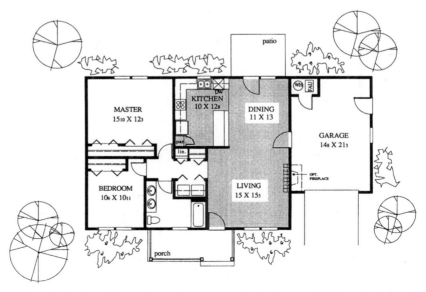

Figure 8.3 For starter homes in ranch markets, a popular design is a fully integrated *community component* consisting of living/dining/kitchen, all in one open vaulted space.

The design of the master suite of any *Group I* home should provide the feeling of being away from it all, but this quality is particularly vital in households that include young children. Although most adults may wish for a sense of order and serenity on the home front, those with children can rarely establish it and almost never sustain it. The need for retreat from chaos is vital and is best satisfied with a master suite that says, "adults only," despite the realities of parenthood that include invasions of this space.

The location of the master suite in young *Group I* households should reflect two seemingly conflicting goals: (1) *privacy from children,* and (2) *immediate access to children.*

For either one- or two-story plans designed for young families, the concept of a *bedroom wing* is most sensible. In two-story plans, a downstairs master bedroom is not preferred by parents of young children, as this location creates logistical problems when there is sickness, sibling rivalry, or just the ordinary commotion of bedtime. Therefore, the options include having a single-level wing locating the master bedroom on the opposite side of the floor plan, since the distance between the two areas will not be substantial unless the home is quite large. Buffer zones for privacy between these two bedroom elements can also be established by placing the baths between the adults' and children's bedrooms or by using an abbreviated hallway. (Figures 8.4 and 8.5)

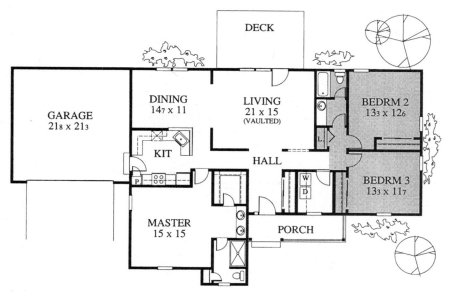

Figure 8.4 For young families in ranch plan markets, a remote bedroom wing for children can be very desirable.

Figure 8.5 In some two-story starter house plans, a typical young-family design locates the master bedroom or suite on one side of the hall and the secondary bedrooms on the other.

With more space allotted to community components and the privacy core, the ceremonial component of a home for young families will account for a lower proportion of total available square footage. To compensate for space limitations, the entry, living, and dining area may become one large space, with function defined by varied floor and ceiling treatments, and a sense of formality established by higher ceilings and focal features such as tall windows. The proportions of the open and wall space should promote furnishing for ceremonial rather than active functions. (Figure 8.6)

Figure 8.6 In homes for young families, the ceremonial component may be compressed in size and combined with the foyer to present the perception of a larger space.

For *mature families* within the overall *Group I* profile, the dimensions of the entire home increase, as does the emphasis on the *ceremonial component.* These buyers are more affluent, and their children are generally older. They entertain more frequently, and their desire to make a statement of financial success is stronger. A more formal dining room is therefore highly desirable; the formality includes physical separation from daily living activities. The dining room should look and feel self-contained with distinctive features that may include French doors opening to a hallway, unique windows and/or lighting treatments, and/or built-in shelves.

For mature *Group I* households, larger dimensions in the living area can offer both impressive ceremonial spaces and more intimate and inviting seating areas for small groups within large social gatherings. A semiprivate conversation alcove in a bay window and a fireplace are appealing focal points, and interior design treatments could emphasize elegance for either feature. (Figure 8.7)

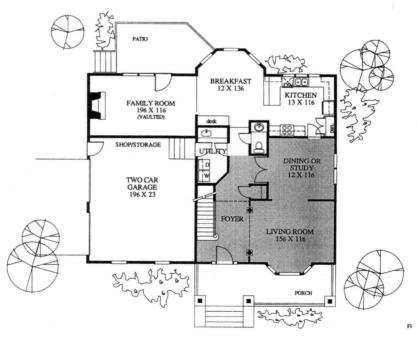

Figure 8.7 For mature families, the dimensions of ceremonial component rooms are increased, and rooms have more definition between one another.

The *community component* for move-up homes remains extremely important, but because these homes are larger, they can incorporate a kitchen design that allows for even more simultaneous activities. Siblings in this household are capable of preparing snacks and simple meals, and they may insist on doing so even when the adult cooks are trying to orchestrate an elegant dinner. A *second sink* with as much *counter space* as possible is most helpful for this subgroup. The family area for move-up buyers is also larger and more elaborate, with a *wet bar,* as well as a highly refined media area that includes a big-screen television set and a built-in sound system. (Figure 8.8)

Figure 8.8 The typical move-up home has a highly developed family room with a good relationship to the kitchen and outdoor spaces.

Mature families are also likely to want an even more informal rec room for games such as table tennis, billiards, and so on. This room is most likely in an improvable lower-level basement. Otherwise, it is most often located over the garage. In either event, noise isolation and a degree of remoteness from privacy areas are highly desirable, because the obvious functions of the room will be noisy. (Figures 8.9 and 8.10)

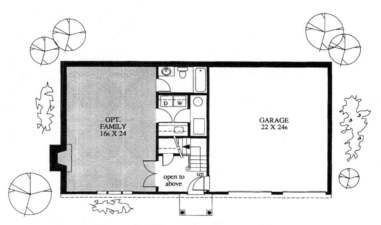

Figures 8.9 (top), 8.10 (bottom) Mature families want a "rec room" for games and activities. Popular locations include the second floor above the garage or a lower-level basement.

Arrangements for the privacy component for mature families will allow for more separation between the master suite and the children's quarters; in two-story plans, the master suite can be on the ground level; in one-story plans, the master and children's rooms can be on opposite sides of the common areas. In move-up homes for mature families, the master suite is generated with the same "adults only" premise but with amenities that can include a fireplace, a seating alcove, and a larger and more elaborate dressing and bath area. (Figure 8.11)

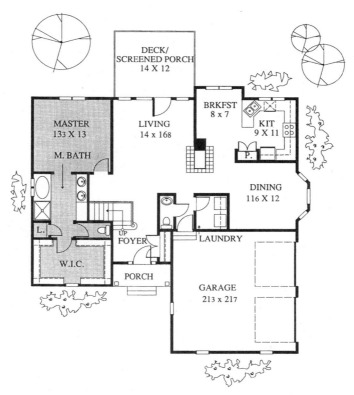

Figure 8.11 Mature buyers are more likely to opt for plans with a first-floor master suite and the secondary bedrooms upstairs.

Mature families will also desire more *storage capability* in the functional component. Most homeowners in this profile groups are still acquiring and keeping new possessions for themselves and are many years away from reducing the volume to fit it into the more compact dimensions of move-down homes. Although older parents in this profile may be fast approaching empty-nester status, many are accommodating some storage requirements of adult or nearly adult children who have not yet established a permanent residence.

Mature families are more likely to also want a separate guest suite in the privacy component. For extended stays of relatives or other family friends, the guest suite may be very necessary. In a household's life cycle, grown children are also known to return to the nest. If so, a separate guest suite, perhaps even with a separate outdoor entrance, is desirable. (Figure 8.12)

Figure 8.12 Mature buyers generally prefer spacious guest suites for extended stays of relatives or friends.

Group II: Couples Without Children

Married people without children generally fall into one of two secondary categories: *relatively young professional couples,* who may or may not be planning to have children later, and *older couples* who never had children, or whose offspring have sprung—the "empty nesters."

In terms of purchasing power, households without children generally are affluent (called DINKS—double income/no kids), so although they are not all technically moving up to larger spaces, they, too, *are seeking a much different product than a starter home.* They may want many of the same elements and amenities demanded by move-up buyers, but they want these amenities in *more compact and manageable components.*

Separate ceremonial and community components are much less important for *Group II* households than for family buyers. The desire or need for a separate family area is greatly diminished; this type of space will be used infrequently even for grandparents, and it will be used for finite time intervals, so it can be scaled down to become an open extension of the kitchen/breakfast area. A larger breakfast nook is desirable, and because it doesn't have to accommodate children, this area can incorporate more formal features and finishes, such as carpeting on the floor. (Figure 8.13)

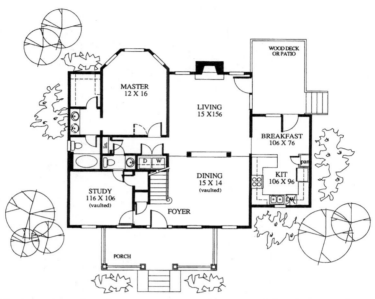

Figure 8.13 Empty-nesters often do not regard separate ceremonial and community components as necessary. Instead, they prefer to combine the square footage into larger rooms.

For *Group II* buyers, the *ceremonial component* receives major emphasis. A separate and formal dining room is appealing to either young or mature buyers in Group II but is probably more important to senior buyers, particularly in traditional markets. The wet bar and formal fireplace favored by move-up buyers are even more desirable to single buyers, particularly as a sophisticated means of enriching relatively smaller square footage. The living room or great room for these affluent buyers may be smaller than that for move-up buyers, but its design should lean more toward formal than to casual function. (Figure 8.14)

The privacy component for *Group II* buyers should reflect the fact that secondary bedrooms are more often used by guests than by the immediate family. In two-story homes for couples without children , a well-appointed ground-floor master suite will attract mature couples. (Figure 8.15) For this group,

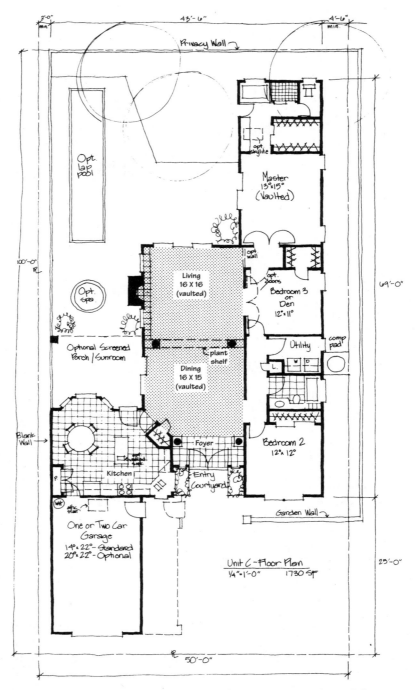

Figure 8.14 *Grand rooms* that combine living and dining rooms are favored for many empty-nester plans.

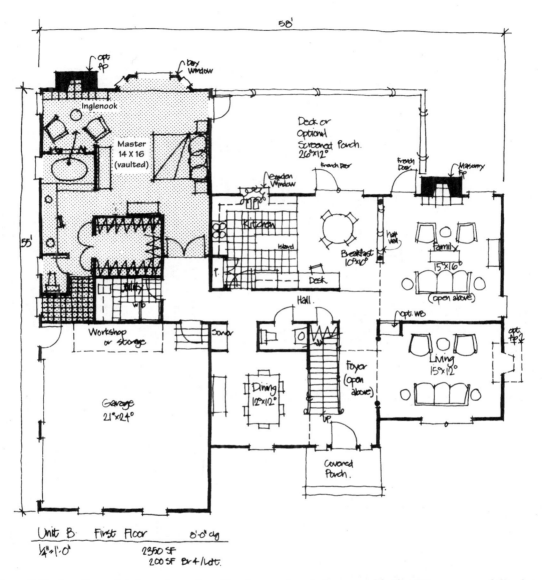

Figure 8.15 A well-appointed master suite with a luxury dressing room and bath, sitting area, and fireplace will attract mature couples without children.

the number of secondary bedrooms may shrink to only one or two; a den that converts easily to guest quarters can augment these bedrooms and might be located on the first floor for flexible use as a home office as well. (Figure 8.16)

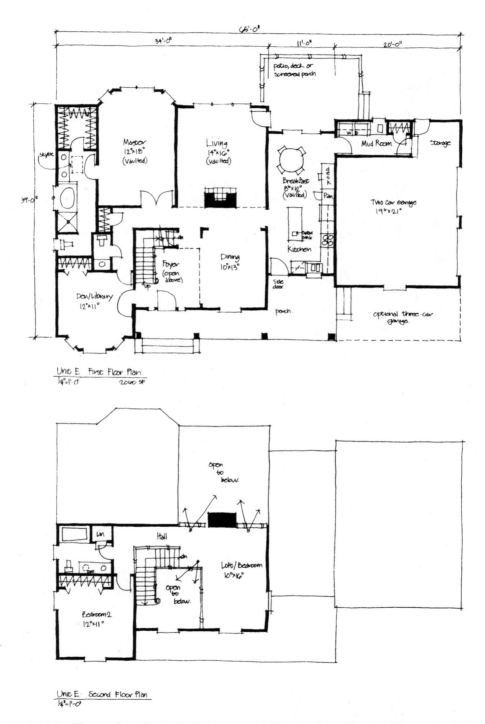

Unit E   First Floor Plan
1/4"=1'-0"   2040 SF

Unit E   Second Floor Plan
1/4"=1'-0"

Figure 8.16 The number of extra bedrooms required for couples without children may shrink to one or two. Locating one off the foyer as a home office is also ideal.

Luxurious baths are part of the package for couples without children, but programs for older couples should consider potential mobility problems. Although a spa tub may be appreciated, it should be easy to enter. Showers should be of the walk-in variety with low curbs, and may include a shelf wide enough to sit on. Indeed, the entire house should be designed for universal accessibility.

Groups III and IV: Single Heads of Household

As mentioned earlier, single buyers come in ever-increasing varieties and ages. The most distinctive variations in design for these buyers will result from considerations of age and parental status.

Younger singles without children are most often first-time buyers, and a single income may dictate attached housing, as discussed in Chapter 9. *Older singles,* particularly women, may also choose attached housing for greater convenience, lower maintenance, and higher security. An increasing number of single buyers, however, are also choosing single-family, detached homes.

Some single buyers may seek either a co-owner or a renter, so they can afford to own a detached house. This cohabitant may be related to the buyer or be a relative stranger. In any case, a design that includes *separate but equal privacy components* can be of great assistance in preventing friction between two unrelated adults sharing the same home. These *dual master* plans can be incorporated into either one or two-story plans, and, for programs geared to higher incomes, can be a design that adds certain amenities found in small apartments. (Figure 8.17)

Each master suite, for example, may offer space and plumbing for a stacked laundry unit. A seating alcove may incorporate a wet bar with cold storage. Each may open to a private deck or patio. Including such features extends the dual privacy component, providing not only the physical separation that mingles require, but also a range of uses that contribute to a feeling of autonomy.

In the community component for mingle buyers, the *kitchen* is the most important element. The design for more affluent buyers could include *separate but equal food preparation and storage areas.* For those with more modest means, partial separation, such as that provided by work islands, is better than none at all.

Unless price is no object, homes for single buyers will usually offer smaller square footages than move-up designs with the emphasis on components dictated by whether or not the buyers have children. Single parents need a community component for play and gathering space as well as privacy and separation from children. Singles without children may need less privacy, and therefore prefer that more space be devoted to the ceremonial component. Age is again the dominant factor in this determination. Most young singles work full-time and may not have the time or inclination to undertake as much formal entertaining as their older counterparts. Conversely, older buyers express a more decided preference for traditional ceremonial spaces.

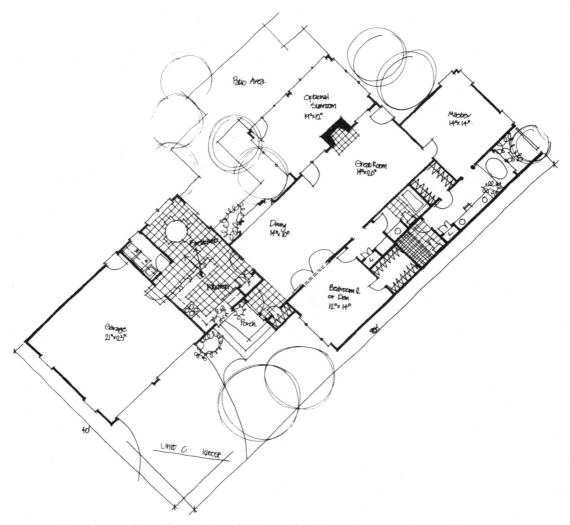

Figure 8.17 Floor plans for "mingle" buyers should provide separate but equal master suites.

A separate family room is generally not desirable for singles without children, nor is a large breakfast room. The kitchen dimensions should accommodate a breakfast area, however, and the space gained by eliminating or abbreviating these spaces can be dedicated to more elaborate master suites or larger living and dining areas.

For singles with or without children, a *home office* option should be considered. Self-employment or *home employment* continues to gain popularity in the American working environment. For many young mothers, a home office represents the ideal way to juggle the need for income with the desire to tend to children. With adequate, affordable child care unavailable to many, home employment becomes even more attractive. Generally, this solution will divert space from the ceremonial component and add it to the community area. This type of arrangement affords a place for single parents who are not working for a paycheck to take care of domestic business and still remain accessible to children. (Figure 8.18)

Figure 8.18 Floor plans with a study or home-office option off the foyer are highly desirable for working single parents.

The diversity of today's buyer profiles could easily generate an entire book devoted to an adequate description of today's new households and market niches. The above discussion provides only an overview of the most significant differences among household profiles and their effect on individual components, as well as the relative status of these components within the overall floor plan. Although they are important starting points, the elements discussed here should be combined with a thorough examination of local market preferences before a final program is adopted.

The most important design issues in any residential design, however, must be decided by remembering that *universal needs and desires prevail over all variables*. Special features will not make amends for lack of function and grace in other components; design that responds to lifestyle considerations for everyone must be the principal ingredient of the residential recipe.

9

Multifamily Considerations: Less Is More

Although they are a well-established form of housing in cities, attached dwellings often have been considered somewhat out of place in suburban and rural American communities. Their postwar use was primarily for rental apartments or to achieve the higher density and smaller square footage requirements of affordable housing. (Figure 9.1) Attached housing recently expanded its role with programs in all price ranges receiving far more design attention than those developed as recently as 15 years ago.

In terms of design emphasis, attached housing now enjoys nearly as much status as detached housing with new attached homes including more creative solutions to the constraints of multifamily housing. The objectives include incorporating more immediate and long-term value features that appeal to a wider range of market profiles. In addition to first-time household buyers, the typical multifamily markets include single renters and buyers of varying age and income ranges, empty-nester couples, and retirees. Luxury attached lifestyle programs have also grown in number and popularity in many geographical areas. (Figures 9.2 and 9.3)

Figure 9.1   Early postwar attached housing was often out of place in suburban or rural American communities.

Figure 9.2   Attached housing has expanded from its traditional role of affordable rental housing to include many other market groups.

Multifamily-Buyer Profiles

Households who elect to purchase or lease multifamily housing are still a minority in the U.S. housing market. Generally, multifamily housing accounts for 15 to 30 percent of all new housing production, and those who buy these homes have sound reasons for their preference. Chief among the advantages is *lower maintenance responsibilities* with exteriors and common areas carried out by others at the direction of a homeowners' association. Affluent empty-nesters want to spend more time traveling and entertaining—and less time on yard work and painting. Older buyers may no longer be physically capable of these chores, and young singles or couples very often don't have the time.

Security is another important attraction of attached housing. A strong sense of neighborhood often develops with attached housing; physical proximity promotes interaction, even if only for the reason that one cannot avoid it! With that interaction comes a keener awareness of cooperative living, which fosters mutual caretaking and a degree of attention to our neighbors that is not always found in detached housing. This mutual concern makes some aspects of daily living more convenient and less isolated, contributing to real and perceived security. (Figure 9.3)

The full potential of multifamily housing, however, can be realized only through superior design and planning. Both floor plans and site plans must provide a sense of high quality. Everyone wants a home to be proud of and a home that lives well, regardless of price or lifestyle.

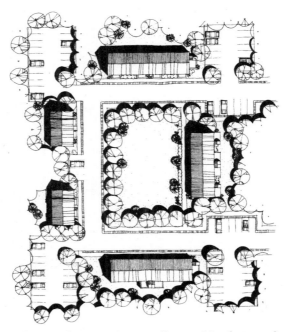

Figure 9.3 A heightened sense of security is generally a positive feature of attached housing communities. In this site plan, open greens are used to promote the use of common space.

Multifamily Design Considerations

Although market groups and buyer attitudes regarding attached housing have changed, some design and planning constraints associated with this residential form have remained constant. They include:

1. *Common walls, loss of privacy, and noise pollution.*
2. *Remote parking and access issues.*
3. *Square-footage and floor plan limitations.*
4. *Stacked living quarters and deck and patio areas (on garden units).*

Thus, designing attached homes involves more compromises than designing detached homes, and mitigating these constraints effectively requires even more design innovation and careful thought.

The interior limitations on the components of attached housing design most often revolve around smaller square footages and common walls. A 700- to 1200-square-foot home physically cannot accommodate all the components and features found in the ideal move-up, detached home. In multifamily homes, the "room with a view" may be only one or two selected rooms within a component. The components themselves will often be blended to define their multiple-use character, and some elements of each component may be abbreviated or eliminated.

Smaller and Open Plans

In multifamily housing design, *open planning* will provide design assistance. For most programs, downsizing is best achieved by "opening the interior envelope"—or removing walls and consolidating rooms within components without compromising their visual appeal or practical function. (Figure 9.4)

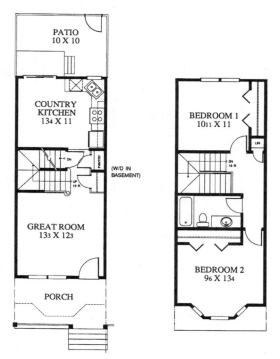

Figure 9.4 Components of attached housing are combined and compressed by the need to build within smaller square footages. This plan is divided into two components on each floor.

With the open-plan approach, the ceremonial component most often becomes a single, large space. A true entry/foyer is eliminated, with the arrival area defined instead by a platform, sculptural ceiling treatment, low abbreviated wall, or other element. Flooring material here may contrast with the floor cover in the rest of the space, further differentiating the point of entry from other elements in the ceremonial component. (Figure 9.5)

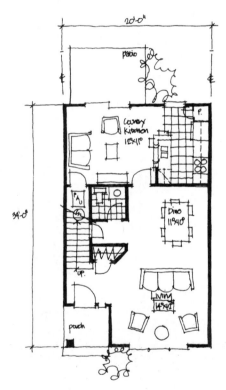

Figure 9.5 This attached home plan used the open-plan approach to minimize interior walls and expand interior space.

Living and dining areas become just that—*areas*—with the goal of providing a feeling of as much space as possible while simultaneously defining the space as ceremonial. As with the entry area, varied ceiling treatments, different floor materials, and low walls add definition; fireplaces and soffits add focus and interest; and unbroken sight lines to the outdoors contribute to a sense of expansion.

Blending Community and Ceremonial Components

Because of square-footage limitations, the area devoted to ceremonial functions may also have to serve as the more casual community component, further testing design ingenuity. Programming for multiple uses dictates that particular attention is paid to the primary functional element of the community component—the *kitchen*. It must relate to areas that will be put to both formal and informal uses.

If the kitchen remains open to living and dining, a raised counter where the kitchen joins these areas is virtually a must. (Figure 9.6) Gracious evening meals are not promoted by a clear view of the remains of the food preparation area. This countertop area can also serve as a breakfast/snack bar—a space-saving and convenient island in our eat-and-run society.

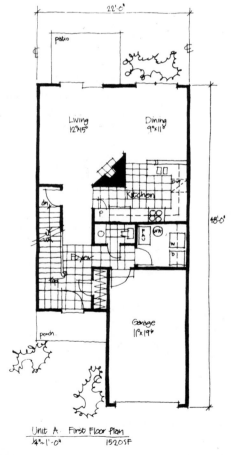

Figure 9.6 In small, multifamily floor plans, the kitchen must relate to both formal and informal uses; thus, an open kitchen should have a raised counter for separation from the living and dining areas.

The kitchen should also incorporate as generous dimensioning as the program allows. Except for the most formal affairs, socializing before and after dinner often includes having guests in the kitchen; even if the kitchen is small, people invariably head for the center of activity and cooking aromas, so creating room where one can maneuver in a crowd is a plus every cook can appreciate.

Capturing Outdoor Space and Views

Opening the ceremonial and community components to a *private outdoor space* is also a very effective way to create a perception of larger square footage. Views to an outdoor deck or patio are not only visually pleasing, but their access and use expands the indoor area. Multifamily plans with *undulating exterior walls* will help to capture more "window walls" that will help bring more natural light and views into the smaller interior spaces. When formal and informal components are combined into one large area, the outdoor spaces usually open from the living/dining area. (Figure 9.7)

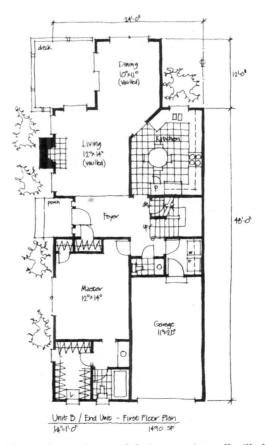

Figure 9.7 This attached home plan with an undulating exterior wall will allow more of the community component to view the outdoors.

Using the Vertical Dimension

As with most housing designs, the design of two-story attached homes reserves the upstairs for privacy components and the downstairs for the community component. In floor plans that have footprints wide enough to include a first-floor bedroom, *dual master suites* with one bedroom located up and one down should be considered. This configuration is appealing for a variety of market groups, including older buyers who prefer ground-floor living; unrelated owners who share a mortgage; empty-nesters with adult children coming to visit; and nearly anyone who has overnight guests. (Figure 9.8)

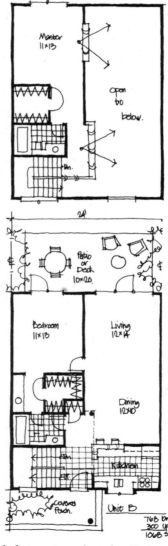

Figure 9.8 For markets that include two-story plans, locating one bedroom down and one up in a "dual master" layout is highly marketable for "mingles."

Other vertical programming to consider includes the placement of volume space. In the same scenario (one bedroom up/one down), there may be an opportunity to introduce volume spaces over the lower community component. This will further enhance the plan to certain lifestyle buyers who value the drama of volume space in a smaller interior.

Efficient Privacy Components

What happens to the privacy components in the compressed dimensions of a very small townhouse or condominium plan?

If two or more bedroom/bath elements comprise the privacy component, locating them on opposite sides of the social areas is highly desirable. If this solution is impractical, then locating the bedrooms on either side of the bathroom or bathrooms is preferable to a bedroom/bedroom/bath configuration. (Figure 9.9)

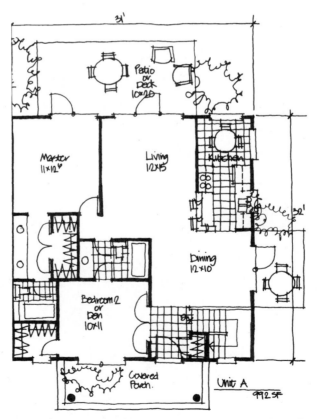

Figure 9.9 For attached-home ranch plans, bedrooms located on opposite ends of the community component are preferred. The secondary bath generally serves as the powder room as well.

Almost all multifamily buyers report a preference for *two* bathrooms. When this is not possible, special care must be assigned to the location of the single bathroom. If the home has one bedroom and one bath, the bath should have *two entrances* for direct private accessibility from both the bedroom and the community component; if space limitations preclude establishing some distance between the master and the social areas, the design should at least guarantee that visitors and guests will not be traversing the privacy component to reach the bath. (Figure 9.10)

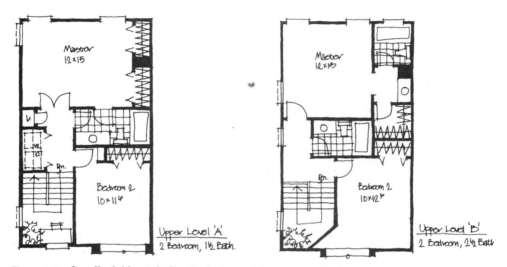

Figure 9.10 In affordable multifamily designs with two or more bedrooms sharing a bath, it is always preferable to give the master bedroom direct access to the bath. If possible, two separate baths are optimal for all market groups.

Because the baths in attached housing will most often be located around a central plumbing core, the bathroom usually has no window. For baths of any size, *a skylight* alleviates this problem. Recessed lighting also helps to expand the space by keeping walls and ceilings uncluttered.

Diminished Scale

When all amenities are accommodated in smaller square footages, scale and proportion are extremely important considerations. Fireplaces, cabinets, beams, soffits, and wall forms must all be scaled for the smaller dimensions found in most attached homes. These reduced dimensions usually can benefit from the introduction of vaulted ceilings—and can be further enriched with features such as ceiling fans, special window treatments, and built-in shelves. The positive appeal of smaller spaces can also be enhanced by balancing these special features precisely and using high-quality materials and finishes. (Figure 9.11)

Figure 9.11 Smaller multifamily interiors must be enriched with features to enhance the diminished scale of the space.

The Outdoor Component

Exterior design for attached housing must concentrate on privacy and individual identity. Site planning should provide at least partial privacy from one unit to another with buildings oriented to preclude direct views from one home to another. Jogging the common walls, both vertically and horizontally, juxtaposing one-story with two-story units to vary roof lines, varying the location of open space between units, and creating back-to-back building configurations are among the many solutions developed to address the privacy needed in attached housing. (Figure 9.12)

Figure 9.12 The exterior design of multifamily housing should strive to individualize the units and provide privacy.

Entry doors should be covered and separated. Landscaping that may include shrubbery or vine-covered trellises is also useful for framing entryways. In stacked programs, a private ground-floor entry and interior stairway to the second-story homes is very desirable. Where inclement weather is often a factor, this entry represents the ideal spot for temporarily parking wet coats, boots, and pets. In any climate, an enclosed ground-level entry adds significantly to the privacy of the entire home and to the sense of progression to living areas that is more often associated with detached homes. (Figure 9.13)

Figure 9.13 In any climate, ground-level entrances add to the privacy and security of a multifamily house.

Accommodating Automobiles

Of all the constraints on designs for attached homes, the one that most impacts its sales appeal is *parking*. Direct access from living quarters to a garage is attractive to all market groups, for obvious reasons. Whether one is loading or unloading a car, close proximity to interior spaces makes the task seem easier than the prospect of traveling to and from remote parking. Security is also a major factor, and although single women may be more adamant about security, all markets prefer immediate access to their cars. (Figure 9.14)

When attached garages cannot be achieved, common access from either enclosed or open parking areas must be considered. Again, convenience and proximity are the key issues. Outdoor grade-level parking should be close to the front entrance. This need may have to be balanced with community design issues, however, because putting parking spaces directly in front of front doorways is highly unsightly. Parking places close to but to the side of the entry are recommended.

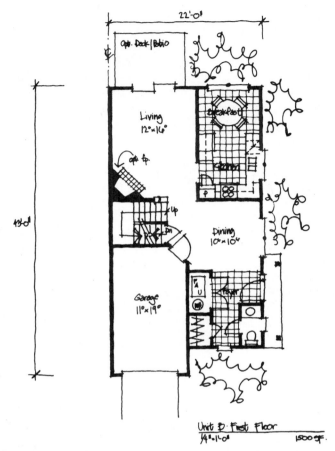

Figure 9.14 Direct access to a garage is highly desirable in multifamily programs if pricing and budgets will permit.

Architects and planners are now achieving densities of up to 30 units per acre in building blocks that include *garages with direct access to the home.* Where density or cost requirements preclude this, designers must utilize other building concepts to resolve the parking issue. These may include free-standing, detached garages remote from the main building, underground parking located directly below the building, or grade-level surface parking near individual entrances.

The Functional Component

Like the other components in attached housing, the spaces devoted to functional use must be compromised to a certain extent. But residents of attached housing have the same if not more need for storage as other households and will be attracted to designs that provide as much interior storage space as possible. Remember that the small floor plans of multifamily designs mean that storage is even more important, as extra rooms and closets probably are not available. Attached-home residents also appreciate additional storage incorporated into the garage or carport. Individual laundry facilities are also important; interior placement of compact washer/dryer combinations is far preferable to centralized facilities.

Conclusion

Incorporating sophisticated design into attached housing is helping to establish the appeal of attached housing in diverse markets. Today's buyers and renters demand much more than "stacked flats" before committing to a residence, and this pressure has generated remarkable innovations in attached-housing design. (Figure 9.15)

Although the attached home may never become the preferred choice for a majority of our population, it has been, and will continue to be, a viable prototype to reduce land and development costs, thereby increasing affordability. As land costs continue to increase, these considerations will become even more significant, and attached housing will continue to gain popularity with buyers of means or certain lifestyle objectives.

Figure 9.15 Design innovation in postwar attached housing has increased its appeal to much broader market groups.

10

Future Trends

As evidenced by any historical review of housing, the continuing evolution of residential design is marked by a double vision: We look back in time to incorporate the forms still valid for modern use; we look forward to create new forms and elements that reflect living needs for the future. Thus, the discussion of *lifestyle design* and *components for living* is incomplete without consideration of trends that may carry into the future for builders and buyers.

What trends will we see in housing design in the future? Like all design, future trends will be driven by changing demographics; perhaps the most important is the increased number of women in the work force. The backbone of the housing market will continue to be trade-up or move-up buyers, for the most part comprising two wage-earning heads of household. Therefore, the average house size is expected to increase, except for empty-nester homes.

The future of housing design is in niche markets. Virtually all builders recognize that the mass-market, cookie-cutter approach is obsolete. Further, smaller lots and more two-story homes will reflect the ongoing increase in land costs. Other major influences on design will be based on income, values, and other concerns.

Affordability

Building costs recently have surged to the forefront of home builder concerns. Spiraling increases in the cost of improved land and building materials have forced home prices higher and higher, with many Americans now priced out of the market. Combined with an increased focus on the national debt and the trade imbalance, this has encouraged the American psyche to shift toward precautionary spending practices. Like government, households must begin to live within their means.

Home builders are responding by assessing the ways they can produce an attractive home in a smaller container. Component design can help determine which rooms should be downsized or eliminated. From this process, new versions of the starter housing and modest move-up homes will emerge in the future. (Figure 10.1)

Figure 10.1 New versions of starter housing will continue to emerge in the future. Smaller lots, such as this 3600-square-foot lot, will certainly be part of that formula.

The primary way to increase affordability is to promote the use of smaller lots and more reasonable street improvement standards. (Figure 10.2) Designing smaller homes that have expansion potential, with basic but upgradable specifications, is another means of reducing home prices. Builders should be cautious, however, about returning to the basic box concept seen at Levittown and other early postwar prototypes of affordable housing. Rightly, builders are scaling back rather than slashing to trim costs and are working to maintain as much aesthetic appeal as possible.

Figure 10.2 The most effective ways to reduce housing costs is through more reasonable site development standards and smaller lots.

Traditionalism

American culture currently is permeated with nostalgia, and more and more home buyers are seeking traditional designs in housing and interior furnishings. This glorification of "days gone by" may indicate that the baby boomers are coming to terms with the aging process, or it may simply be a resurgence of the age-old habit of fondly recalling the past. (Figure 10.3)

Traditionally styled elevations have always been more popular than contemporary exteriors, but the current emphasis on traditionalism also includes an interest in community planning concepts that recall older streetscapes. In sunbelt markets, after years of attention to narrow-lot schemes, the "wide-and-shallow" lot pattern is gaining momentum because of its streetscape appeal.

Figure 10.3 The trend toward traditionalism in new home design is evidenced by the ongoing popularity of traditionally styled elevations.

Planning schemes for new communities are emulating small towns as desirable prototypes. In the future, community developers will also include more of the traditional amenities of a small town, such as more common greens, neighborhood retailers, sidewalks, and recreational amenities, as well as diverse housing types. (Figure 10.4)

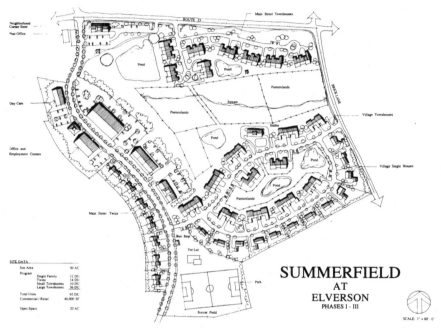

Figure 10.4 More new communities are being planned with traditional small towns as models—with mixed uses and diverse housing types.

Buyers will be attracted to house designs that use traditionally popular materials and details, as well as quality interior materials, such as hardwood floors, wood windows, and solid-wood cabinets. At the same time, these buyers will continue to demand maximum function and practicality for contemporary use. The interior components of even the most traditional house must continue to respond to the many facets of current American lifestyles.

Environmentalism

Awareness of and concern for the state of our environment is still growing. Not since the first Earth Day in 1970 has so much attention been focused on our natural surroundings, and never before have we seen such a high level of consumer activism.

With mandatory recycling already in effect in major cities, waste management is certain to become a significant design theme. Currently, homes allow for recycling activities, with areas for the separation, storage, and processing of solid wastes located in the functional component. A key issue to be resolved will be *ease of recycling.* Today, even minimal recycling efforts, such as those devoted to newspapers, bottles, and cans, involve storing these materials until the accumulated volume justifies the time spent in bundling, bagging, and hauling the materials to a center that may be many miles away. In most busy households, these efforts are viewed as laudable but easy to forego. If future designs can make such processes easier, participation in this type of environmental preservation will undoubtedly increase. (Figure 10.5)

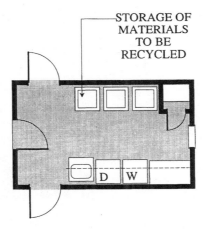

RECYCLE CENTER IN MUDROOM

Figure 10.5 One example of the increased concern for environmental quality is the emergence of home recycling centers.

Resource conservation is also an increased concern. Water-saving devices for toilets and showers, in place in much of our new housing, may be augmented with recycling mechanisms for some wastewater once such technology can be affordably incorporated. Low-use dishwashers that use only 6 gallons of water instead of the usual 16 gallons are currently available. Ground-source heat pumps, double-paned windows, and thicker exterior super-insulated walls will all become standard. Heating and cooling systems will be multiple zoned and fitted with electronic supervisory controls to reduce energy consumption. Microwave clothes dryers will soon be available along with point-of-source heating for hot water (so you don't have to waste water in the shower until the hot water shows up!).

Home gardening is another aspect of environmental awareness and is growing in popularity. As well as being a form of relaxation, gardening satisfies an instinctive human desire to "live off the land." The component design of single-family lots can easily integrate the gardening movement into the outdoor component, and we may see the integration of communal gardens in multifamily programs. Traditionally, high-density, inner-city neighborhoods have included communal gardening of infill parcels, and in the future, we may see similar activities in suburban garden apartments or condominiums. (Figure 10.6)

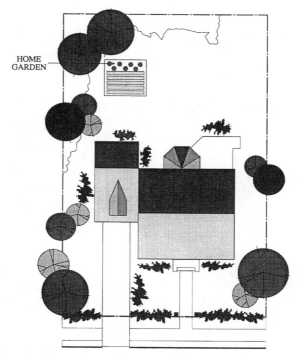

Figure 10.6 The interest in home gardening is another response to the sustainable community movement.

Land planning and design for solar consideration is also regaining popularity. Although not as pervasive a design theme as in the 1970s, solar heating is by no means a dead issue, and recognition of passive solar benefits is on the upswing. Using glass walls along southern exposures, for example, is a feasible planning gesture that can enhance either the ceremonial or community component while it reduces fuel consumption. (Figure 10.7)

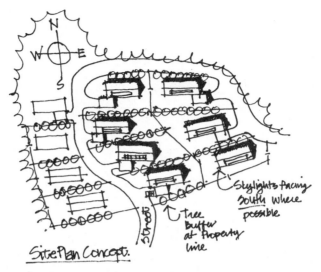

Figure 10.7 In the future, land planning of production home communities will become sensitive to solar orientations.

Health

Our culture is infatuated with food but, happily, seems to be equally concerned with personal health and fitness. Lifestyle housing must address the major issues of access to indoor and outdoor recreational facilities.

In a single-family home, this trend is addressed with lap swimming pools and the integration of exercise rooms or areas into either the privacy or the community component. In multifamily programs, community health and fitness activities are provided for by recreational facilities that have become the focus of on-site amenities. (Figure 10.8)

Figure 10.8 Community fitness centers will become more and more common in both single and multifamily neighborhoods.

More indirect reflections of the emphasis on health and fitness can be seen in the kitchen and bath areas. The importance of eating the right foods means more time is spent in purchasing, storing, and preparing foods. Larger and more elaborate bathing and dressing areas respond to the emphasis on cleanliness in environments akin to those found in health spas. In the future, an additional full third bath will become more common than today's two-and-a-half bath home.

Socialization

In terms of its effect on housing design, this factor may be the most remote, but the influence of our need for social companionship is real. The dominance of technology in the workplace has reduced people-oriented tasks. Most personal banking transactions, for example, are handled by computer rather than by warm-blooded tellers. Businesses that provided home delivery—of groceries, medical care, and other services—have virtually disappeared. Our society has become more isolated and less social.

The impact of this is reflected in the privatization of homes. The past decade has included a decline in streetscape quality and community design, particularly in areas with high land costs. New housing has placed a stronger emphasis on interior elements, with minimal attention paid to the curb elevation.

But people are again embracing the notion of community, and buyers are anxiously seeking welcoming neighborhoods where they can develop new friendships and preserve the closeness of family. So the pendulum is swinging back toward traditional, small-town streetscapes and front porches seen in the wide-and-shallow lot patterns discussed earlier. (Figure 10.9)

Figure 10.9 Community planning and residential design will continue to focus on concepts that promote quality neighborhoods and socialization.

Conclusion

The component method of design provides a framework for planning the house itself, one that can be integrated with diverse and particular lifestyle details. It also applies to the broader issues of values and serves as a valid starting point for achievement of the most important synthesis of all—one that balances home, resources, and community to fulfill our contemporary needs and create a positive environment for daily life.

Illustration Credits

All uncredited photographs and illustrations in the book were created by the author. The following is a list of figures that resulted from commissioned designs. The listings include the project name, location, and client. (The location and client are given only with the first mention of a project.)

Figure 1.5	Diamond Lake; Glastonbury, CT; Havenwood Homes
Figure 1.6	McConnell; Davidson, NC; Crosland Land Company
Figure 1.7	The Meadows at Riverbend; Middletown, CT; Real Estate Service of Connecticut
Figure 1.8	The Meadows at Riverbend
Figures 1.14, 1.15, 1.16, 1.17	Spring Ridge; Wyomissing, PA; Peter Carlino Companies
Figure 1.19	Downing Woods; Chapel Hill, NC; Hoying and Huff
Figure 2.27	Wheatstone; Lancaster, PA; Charter Homes
Figure 3.1	Spring Ridge
Figure 3.3	Capewoods; Cape May, NJ; Bowman Builders
Figure 3.4	Treyburn; Durham, NC; Cimarron Homes
Figure 3.30	Custom Residence; Elverson, PA
Figure 4.1	Spring Ridge
Figure 4.2	Country Gates; Wilmington, DE; Gilman Properties
Figure 5.1	Spring Ridge
Figure 6.9	Wickford Point; Wickford, RI; Gilbane Properties
Figure 6.10	Hidden Hollow; Durham, NC; Cimarron Homes
Figure 6.11	The Meadows at Riverbend
Figure 6.12	Huntington; Rock Hill, SC; Charlotte Building Group
Figure 6.13	Providence Park at Antigua; Myrtle Beach, SC; MBF Homes
Figure 6.14	McConnell
Figure 6.15	Wickford Point
Figure 6.16	The Meadows at Riverbend
Figure 7.2	The Highlands; Harrisburg, PA; Richmar Builders
Figure 7.3	Wheatstone
Figure 7.4	Spring Ridge
Figure 7.5	McConnell
Figure 7.6	Diamond Lake

Figure 7.8	Summerfield; Elverson, PA; Stoltzfus Enterprises Builders
Figure 7.9	Wickford Point
Figure 7.11	Diamond Lake
Figure 7.12	The Meadows at Durham; Bristol, PA; Capponi & Sons
Figure 7.13	Abbey Downs; Royersford, PA; E.J. Callaghan
Figure 8.1	The Highlands
Figure 8.2	Lenox; Durham, NC; Cimarron Homes
Figure 8.3	Brentwood; Bozeman, MT; Garrity Homes
Figure 8.4	Capewoods
Figures 8.5, 8.6	Hunters Woods; Bethel, PA; Clark Builders
Figure 8.7	McConnell
Figure 8.8	Treyburn
Figures 8.9, 8.10	The Meadows at Riverbend
Figures 8.11, 8.12	Treyburn
Figure 8.13	McConnell
Figure 8.14	Providence Park at Antigua
Figure 8.15	Huntington
Figure 8.16	Summerfield
Figure 8.17	Pinehurst Place at Greenbrier; New Bern, NC; Weyerhaeuser Real Estate
Figure 8.18	McConnell
Figure 9.3	Bentley Ridge; Lancaster, PA; High Associates
Figure 9.4	Misercordia Site; Milwaukee, WI; Firstar Community Reinvestment Corp.
Figure 9.5	The Highlands
Figure 9.6	The Orchards; Mount Joy, PA; Melhorn Development
Figure 9.7	Summerfield
Figures 9.8, 9.9	Northridge; Windham, CT; Schuyler Corporation
Figure 9.10	Castle Hill; Holyoke, MA; Edward Lapidus
Figure 9.11	Coventry Pointe; North Coventry Township, PA; Basile Corporation
Figure 9.12	Summerfield
Figure 9.13	Bentley Ridge
Figure 9.14	Hershey Fields; Hershey, PA; Richmar Builders
Figure 9.15	Summerfield
Figure 10.1	Breckenridge; Durham, NC; Cimarron Homes
Figure 10.2	Downing Woods
Figure 10.3	Old Farm; Middletown, CT; Real Estate Service of Connecticut
Figure 10.4	Summerfield
Figure 10.6	Wickford Point
Figure 10.9	Crystal Meadows; Durham NC; Cimarron Homes

Bibliography

Selected Books About Residential Design

Alexander, Christopher. *A Pattern Language,* New York: Oxford University Press, 1977. A fascinating manifesto based on the theory that designs for cities, as well as for individual homes, can be organized with a collection of time-honored patterns.

_____. *The Production of Houses,* New York: Oxford University Press, 1985. An application of the theories in *A Pattern Language.* Alexander was hired to construct a village in Mexicali, Mexico. This book traces the sequencing of local participation in the design and construction process.

Anthenat, Kathy Smith. *American Tree Houses and Playhouses,* Whitehall, VA: Betterway Publications, Inc. Color illustrations of playhouses for kids.

Architects Small House Service Bureau. *Your Future Home*, Washington, DC: AIA Press, 1992. (Originally published by Weyerhaeuser Forest Products in 1923.)

Baker, John. *American House Styles: A Concise Guide*, New York: Norton, 1994.

Bookout, Lloyd, et. al., eds. *Residential Development Handbook, Second Edition,* Washington, DC: The Urban Land Institute, 1991. A comprehensive guide for residential development.

Chamberlain, S., and J. Pollock. *Fences, Gates and Walls: How to Design and Build,* Los Angeles, CA: HP Books, Price Stern Sloan, Inc., 1983.

Clark, Clifford Edward, Jr. *The American Family Home 1800–1960,* Chapel Hill, NC: University of North Carolina Press, 1986.

Daview, Thomas D., Jr., and Kim A. Beasley, *Fair Housing Design Guide for Accessibility,* Washington, DC: National Association of Homebuilders, 1992.

_____. *Deck Planner: 25 Outstanding Decks You Can Build,* Tucson, AZ: Home Planners, Inc., 1990.

_____. *Early American Home Plans,* Farmington Hills, MI: Home Planners, Inc. A modern-day pattern book by a large, stock-plan service. Includes text describing how historical styles can be adapted to contemporary programs.

Ewing, Reid. *Developing Successful New Communities,* Washington, DC: The Urban Land Institute, 1991. A case study overview of conventional new communities.

Foy, Jessica, and Thomas J. Schlereth, eds. *American Home Life 1880–1930: A Social History of Spaces and Services,* Knoxville, TN: University of Tennessee Press, 1994.

Grady, Wayne. *Green Home: Planning and Building the Environmentally Sound House,* Camden East, Ontario: Camden House Publishing, 1993.

Gutman, Robert. *The Design of American Housing,* New York: Publishing Center for Cultural Resources, 1985. This book explains who is designing our homes and how it is done.

Gowans, Alan. *The Comfortable House, North American Suburban Architecture 1890–1930,* Cambridge, MA: MIT Press, 1986. A scholarly review of the initial suburban building boom. From 1890 to 1930 more homes were built than in the nation's entire history, in styles that included bungalow, saltbox, shingle, tudor, and gothic. These were "comfortable" houses.

Hayden, Delores. *Redesigning the American Dream,* New York: Norton, 1984. An argument for smaller homes for smaller households, many of which comprise single women or mothers.

Hegemann, Werner, and Elbert Peets. *American Vitruvius: An Architect's Handbook to Civic Art*, New York: Princeton Architectural Press, 1992. (Originally published by the Architectural Book Publishing Company in 1922.)

Hirschman, Jessica Elin. *Porches and Sunrooms,* New York: Michael Friedman Publishing Group, 1993. A color idea book.

Jacobson, Max, Murray Silverstein, and Barbara Winslow. *The Good House: A Contrast as a Design Tool,* Newton, CT: The Taunton Press, 1990. A collection of design approaches to satisfy more human and emotional needs in residential architecture, written by the coauthors of *A Pattern Language.*

Jandl, H. Ward. *Yesterday's Houses of Tomorrow: Innovative Homes 1850 to 1950,* Washington, DC: Preservation Press, 1991. A case study look at homes that introduced new ideas about housing.

Jarvis, Frederick D. *Site Planning and Community Design for Great Neighborhoods,* Washington DC: Home Builder Press, 1993.

Jones, Robert T. *Authentic Small Houses of the Twenties,* New York: Dover, 1929 (1987 ed).

Katz, Peter. *The New Urbanism: Toward an Architecture of Community*, New York: McGraw-Hill, 1994.

Kemp, Jim. *American Vernacular,* Washington, DC: AIA Press, 1990. Examines over 50 indigenous styles of American design.

Kendig, Lane. *Performance Zoning,* Washington, DC: Planners Press, 1980. A wonderful argument for basing development controls on performance standards such as floor area ratios and impervious cover, instead of conventional controls such as minimum lot sizes, setbacks, etc.

Kostof, Sprio. *America by Design,* New York: Oxford University Press, 1987. Companion to the PBS television series, this book discusses housing as part of the overall built environment.

Lancaster, Clay. *The American Bungalow, 1880–1930,* New York: Abbeville Press, 1985. Traces the origins of the beloved bungalow, which served as a prototype affordable home for generations.

Langdon, Philip. *American Houses,* New York: Stewart, Tabori & Chang, 1987. A rich color pictorial with insightful commentary on all types of housing.

_____. *A Better Place to Live: Reshaping the Suburb*, Amherst, MA: University of Massachusetts Press, 1994.

McAlester, Virginia, and Lee McAlester. *A Field Guide to American Houses,* New York, NY: Alfred A. Knopf, Inc., 1984. A comprehensive guide to historical residential architecture in America.

Moore, Charles, Gerald Allen, Donlyn Lyndon. *The Place of Houses,* New York: Holt, Rinehart and Winston, 1974. A classic and poetic look at the residential design process.

Moore, Charles, et al. *Home Sweet Home: American Domestic Vernacular Architecture,* New York: Rizzoli International Publications, 1983.

Mohr, Merilyn. *Home Playgrounds,* Scarborough, Ontario: Camden House/Firefly Books, 1988.

Nolon, John R. and Duo Dickenson. *Common Walls/Private Homes,* New York: McGraw-Hill, Inc., 1990. Case studies of successful multifamily prototypes with commentary.

Peason, David. *The Natural House Book: Creating a healthy, harmonious and ecologically sound home environment,* New York: Fireside/Simon and Schuster, 1989. An excellent book on healthy residential design issues.

Prowler, Donald. *Modest Mansions,* Emmaus, PA: Rodale Press, 1985. A practical guide to designing smaller, more modest individual homes.

_____. *Questions and Answers about Building,* Newton, CT: The Taunton Press, Inc., 1989. Published by the same group that produces *Fine Homebuilding* magazine, this book addresses technical details of building homes.

Ramsey, Dan. *Fences, Decks and other Backyard Projects,* Blue Ridge Summit, PA: TAB Books (McGraw-Hill), 1992.

Rybczynski, Witold. *Home, A Short History of an Idea,* New York: Viking Penguin, Inc., 1986. The idea is comfort; this book is a study of comfort as an ideal in house design.

_____. *The Most Beautiful House in the World,* New York: Viking, 1989. The most beautiful house in the world is the house one builds for oneself. This is a book about that process, inspired by the author's own experience.

Schuttner, Scoot. *Building and Designing Decks,* Newtown, CT: Taunton Press, Inc., 1993.

Sherwood, Gerald E. and Robert C. Stroh. *Wood Frame House Construction,* Armonk, NY: Armonk Press, 1988. Available through the NAHB Bookstore, this book is an excellent technical guide to residential construction details.

Stevenson, Katherine Cole and H. Ward Jandl. *Houses by Mail,* Washington, DC: The Preservation Press, 1986. A listing of home designs that were available through Sears, Roebuck and Company from 1908 to 1940.

Stiles, David. *Sheds: The Do-it Yourself Guide for Backyard Builders,* Charlotte, VT: Camden House Publishing, 1993. Includes some great ideas for "accessory structures."

Strombeck, Janet A. and Richard H. Strombeck. *Backyard Structures: Designs and Plans,* Delafield, WI: SunDesigns.

_____. *The Backyard Builder's Book of Outdoor Building Projects,* Emmaus, PA: Rodale Press, Inc., 1987.

Van Buren, Maurie. *House Styles at a Glance,* Atlanta, GA: Longstreet Press, 1991. A guidebook to identify historical housing styles.

Van der Ryn, Sim, and Peter Calthorpe. *Sustainable Communities,* San Francisco, CA: Sierra Club Books, 1986. Along with other contributors, the authors describe environmentally responsible community design issues in the urban and suburban context.

_____. *Venturi Scott Brown & Associates, on Houses and Housing,* New York: St. Martins Press, 1992. A look at how a respected design firm approaches residential commissions.

Walker, Lester. *American Shelter, An Illustrated Encyclopedia of the American Home,* Woodstock, NY: The Overlook Press, 1981. The author explains the history of American housing with detailed sketches and text. A well-researched, comprehensive, unique reference book.

Weaver, Gerald L. *Fireplace Designs,* Cincinnati, Ohio: Betterway Books, 1993.

Wentling, James W. and Lloyd W. Bookout. *Density by Design,* Washington, DC: Urban Land Institute, 1988. A case-study book with new small-lot and multifamily building types.

Wright, Gwendolyn. *Building the Dream: A Social History of Housing in America,* Cambridge, MA: MIT Press, 1981. A unique view of the domestic environment in America, from the New England town, through industrial villages, to suburban sprawl and public housing.

Books and Articles by James Wentling

1988

"Designs Make Tomorrow's Affordable Housing Possible Today," *Multi-Housing News,* May, pp. 36–37.

"Density by Design," *Urban Land,* June, pp. 10–15.

"Small Lot Housing: Innovation or Instant Slums?" *Journal of Real Estate Development.* Winter, Vol. 3, 3, pp. 45–53.

"The Advent of Traditionalism in Community Planning," *Land Development,* December, pp. 23–27.

James W. Wentling and Lloyd W. Bookout, eds. *Density by Design,* Washington, DC: The Urban Land Institute.

1990

"A Simple Formula for Producing Affordable Detached Housing," *Urban Land,* May, pp. 2–5.

"Successful Floor Plans for Small Houses," *The Journal of Light Construction,* October.

1991

"Small Lot Housing Typology," *Progressive Architecture,* June, pp. 45–49.

"Affordability Concerns will Dominate New Rental Housing Designs," *Sun Coast/Architect Builder,* October, pp. 26–28.

1992

"Can we afford not to build 'affordable' housing?" *Tri-State Real Estate Journal,* January 17.

1994

James W. Wentling, *Designing a Place to Call Home: Reordering the Suburbs*, New York: Chapman and Hall.

Articles About James Wentling/Architects

1990

"Small-Lot Magic," (Breckenridge), *BUILDER,* July, pp. 120–121.

"Builders Choice Awards," (Breckenridge), *BUILDER,* October, p. 180.

1991

"Pennsylvania Townhomes Retain Heritage of the Land," (Summerfield at Elverson), *Sun Coast Architect/Builder,* April, pp. 32–33.

"A Townlike Plan Sells in the Suburbs," (Bentley Ridge), *Urban Land,* June, pp. 30–31.

1992

"North by Southwest," (Meadows at Riverbend), *BUILDER,* January, pp. 260–261.

"Traditional Styling Reflected in Compact Zero-Lot-Line Plan," (Stratton Park), *Professional Builder and Remodeler,* January, p. 31.

"Affordability Comes in Regionally Appropriate Dress," (Hidden Hollow), *Sun Coast Architect/Builder,* January, p. 21.

"America's Best Affordable New Homes," (Stratton Park), *Better Homes and Gardens,* May, p. 88.

"Builders Best," (Buckwater Creek), *BUILDER,* July, p. 106.

"Pennsylvania Townhomes Combine Style and Grace with Efficiency," (Coventry Pointe), *Sun Coast Architect/Builder,* November, pp. 18–19.

The American House: Design for Living, (Breckenridge), Washington, DC: AIA Press, pp. 68–69.

1993

"A Window for Architects: James Wentling/Architects," *Philadelphia Architect,* July.

"Massachusetts Law Promotes Mixed Income Housing," (Benton Estates), *Urban Land,* October, pp. 10–11.

1994

"A New Deal," (McConnell at Davidson), *BUILDER,* January, pp. 210–211.

"Affordable Housing, 9 Profiles, Some Responses by Architects," *Inland Architect*, January/February, pp. 27–33.

"Portfolio—McConnell at Davidson," *Land Development,* Spring/Summer, pp. 30–32.

"Builders Choice Awards," (McConnell at Davidson), *BUILDER*, October.

"Leaders of the Pack," (Heritage Fields), *BUILDER*, October.

Index

ABOUT THE AUTHOR

James W. Wentling is the principal of James Wentling/Architects, a Philadelphia firm specializing in residential design and planning. The firm's award-winning portfolio includes a broad range of housing types built in locations throughout the United States.

After receiving a bachelor of architecture degree from the University of Notre Dame, Mr. Wentling interned with several firms in San Diego and Philadelphia. He has served as chair of the AIA Housing Committee, as well as vice president of a Residential Council in the Urban Land Institute. He has lectured on residential design throughout the United States as well as in Canada, Europe, and Asia.